# Letters to My Daughter

One Woman's Journey Back to
Self-Love

Elisa Jane Pool

Copyright ©2024 by Elisa Pool, published by Wellness Effect Press

ISBN-13: 979-8-9901822-1-9

eBook ISBN: 979-8-9901822-0-2

Cover Photo by Jess Veguez Photography

Book Cover Design by Vikaina Pino

# Contents

Dedication                              VI

Epigraph                                VII

Reader's Note                           VIII

Preface                                 XI
Girl & Boy Butts

PART ONE:                               XIX
Collision

1.  Dad's Death                         1

2.  The Gift Grief Gives                10

3.  Beauty from the Ashes               16

PART TWO:                               22
False Foundation

4.  You Don't Matter                    23

5.  Worthless                           33

6.  Freshman Fifteen                    43

7.  Self-Fulfilling Prophecies          49

8.  Shaping Self-Awareness              54

9.  Eager for Adventure                                63

PART THREE:                                            76
Demolition

10.  The Crumbling Chameleon                           77

11.  My Food Matters?                                  85

12.  Sourdough Pancakes                                91

13.  You Can Just Say No                               99

14.  What Do YOU Want?                                 104

15.  Mothers and Daughters                             111

16.  Go Your Own Way                                   120

17.  Beauty is in the Eye of the Beholder              129

PART FOUR:                                             145
Reconstruction

18.  Close Calls                                       146

19.  Attention, Please.                                151

20.  Harvest Time                                      159

21.  Batting Averages                                  171

22.  Food Junkie                                       178

23.  The Comparison Trap                               188

24.  Be On Your Own Team                               202

25.  Yellow Bleeping                                   212

26.  Everything Always Works Out For Us                221

27.  Body Beautiful                                227

Afterword: Words of Love                           236

Ending Epigraph                                    246

Acknowledgments                                    247

About The Author                                   253

Endnotes                                           254

For Athena Jane, to whom I go,
and for Carolyn, from whom I come.


*"Te quiero tanto, tanto, tanto, tanto. Cada día un poco más."*
-Song by OV7


Translation:
"I love you so, so, so, so much.  Every day a little more."

"and i said to my body. softly.
'i want to be your friend.'
it took a long breath. and replied
'i have been waiting my whole life for this."[1]
— Nayyirah Waheed


"i am mine.
before i am ever anyone else's."[2]
— Nayyirah Waheed

# Reader's Note

My daughter's name is Athena, goddess of wisdom, warfare, and craftwork. I didn't choose her name; her father did. He was adamant about that name, and would consider no other option for her. I had no way of knowing how appropriate her name would be for the role she would take in my life.

The goddess Athena knew when and who to fight, as well as for whom to fight. She knew how to create and destroy. She was a strong warrior, a wise advisor, and an astute mastermind, all in one. I would venture to say each of us has an "Athena" inside us, waiting to be called into action. My daughter was the catalyst I needed for my inner goddess to be called forth and break free; perhaps this is yours.

Often, in my letters to my daughter, I say "sweet girl", or "honey," because I'm speaking or writing directly to her. *You* are also that sweet girl. Although you, dear reader, are not *my* daughter, you are someone's daughter, someone's son, someone's child. And therefore, these letters are also for you.

I've organized this book into four sections according to the life journey I've taken so far. Oblivious to my lack of self-love — or even any identity of my own most of my life — I start it with the moment that who I was came crashing down around me, which was my father's death. That section is titled "Collision," which is an appropriate descriptor for both the cause of his death, as well as the metaphorical feeling I experienced in the aftermath.

Once he died, I started unraveling, which was, in retrospect, exactly what I needed. It forced me to look at who I *thought* I was, where I came from, and how the beliefs that were running my life might have been instilled. You'll find that in the second section, "False Foundation."

The next section, "Demolition," is when I was confronted with the outcomes of those beliefs, the person I was at the time, considering which aspects I liked and didn't like about myself, and the possibility that I could actually change who I was.

"Reconstruction," the final section, as you might imagine, is all about the process of rebuilding my identity, learning to love myself, and the perspectives I learned along the way.

Many of the words on these pages are memories — personal to me and the memories I hold of my daughter. You'll discover the memories of my parents woven throughout, because the histories of our parents are intertwined with our futures.

It's a very vulnerable thing, to tell one's story. You're putting yourself in someone else's hands for as long as they choose to hold it. When they have it in their hands, they can do many things with it. They can crush it, or rip it to shreds. They can take what's in it and hurl it back at you. They can examine it closely, or lift it and let it shimmer in the sun. They can cherish and care for it… maybe even share it. Whatever you choose to do with it when it's in your hands, thank you for participating in my story, sweet girl. It is all for you.

# Preface

## Girl & Boy Butts

D ear Athena,
   You don't remember this night, but I do.

I'm on my knees in the bathroom, on the bathmat, in the "Happy House," as you and Michael called it, in Milwaukie, Oregon. It's the only house you've known so far, the one we lived in when you were born, with our sweet dog Hank, before we sold it and began our nomadic adventure.

It's evening bath time, and I'm watching you both in the tub. The tub is half full of warm, clear water. No bubbles this time, but there's a sprinkling of toys, and lots of foam letters — the chunky, capital ones in red, blue, yellow, and green. Some are in the water, but most are plastered against the tile wall opposite the shower curtain, because you kiddos are standing up, facing that wall, busy spelling out our family names. You'd already spelled out both of your names, and were now onto the parents.

"B - E - N - J - O... How do you spell Benjamin?"

I'm admiring your teamwork, and begin noticing your sweet little bodies. Michael's is compact, lean, and wiry. Yours is soft, dense, and thick. My gaze lovingly travels from your heads, along the slope of your neck and shoulders, down your backs, and lands on your cute little bums.

Michael's butt is high and tight, like two baseballs have been implanted under his skin. Your buttcheeks, however, are low and plump, like two squishy throw pillows.

It strikes me how different your little bodies are already, at such young ages — you are one week past your fourth birthday, and Michael is 5 and a half. I adore it so much that I snap a picture with my phone (where it remains), smiling as I think how cute this photo will be for years to come.

In the next instant, my smile vanishes as your futures flash before me: I hear Michael lamenting, "Mom, I'm smaller than *all* the other guys! It doesn't matter that I'm fast." He's been left behind by bigger boys, and girls who think boys should be bigger than they are.

Then I hear you, despairing, "I'm bigger than all the other girls. I'm bigger than YOU, mom!" perpetually worried about your size. I see all the future trauma and pain you could experience, the low self-worth you are feeling, all related to the size and appearance of your own bodies.

I fear for you. I fear for Michael, my handsome son, and I fear for you, my beautiful daughter, because your body type doesn't fit the predominant image of beauty in American media. I hate that I fear this for either of you, and I realize I hate it because my entire life — over 40 years of it — was spent trying to prove I was worth something with the appearance of *my* body. My choices, my perspective, and my sense of self had all been dictated by this belief that I was only as good as my body looked — but I never knew exactly what that was supposed to be, because it was governed by some invisible force, and it kept changing, like a fashion trend.

I never realized how little I loved myself until I was confronted with the shape of your body. It's a good thing I was kneeling on the floor, because the realization hit me like a ton of bricks. I was NOT going to let the same thing happen to you, or to your brother.

In that instant, I saw with crystal clarity how absolutely asinine it is, how foolish, limiting, and uneducated it truly is, to ascribe *any* kind of value or meaning to *any* person based on their body or the way it looks — especially when our bodies are treated like commodities.

I couldn't — I *wouldn't* — let this become a reality for either of you. My sweet, innocent babies happily playing in the tub were far too important to minimize their existence by linking it to their outward appearance. You would *not* become victims to the media. You would *not* be manipulated by people who make millions off the very insecurities they help create.

How would I do it? How would I raise you to resist these pervasive and influential messages? How would I also teach you to resist the messages that say your body doesn't matter at all? How would I teach you to love, respect and honor yourselves, no matter what your bodies became, or were able to do?

I knew from almost 20 years of teaching, and four more working with youth in a different capacity, that the very best way for you to learn was to see it in action. After all, they say that values are "caught" rather than taught. That meant I would have to model it for you.

There was only one problem with that:  *I would have to love myself.*

Even though I was afraid, even though I didn't know *how* to love myself, I began that very moment. I knew I would figure it out. It was never a question, sweet girl, because I knew with everything in my soul that *my* body, *your* body, and *every* body (mom, wife, daughter, niece, aunt, grandma, sister; dad, husband, son, nephew, uncle, grandpa, brother) – your body has *nothing* to do with your worth, but *everything* to do with your life. And I want you to live your life ALL OUT, empowered, playing as large as you possibly can.

That moment changed my relationship with myself, and therefore my relationship with you, with my own mom, and with the world. It changed my calling, as a matter of fact. On that day, unbeknownst to me, the seed for this book was planted. This book is about the journey of self-love; mainly, my journey back to loving myself, and my hope is that you love yourself deeply, the way you did when you were young, your whole life long. It's about the long path home to yourself, a journey I hope every woman takes. I say home, to yourself, because I think it's a round-trip ticket.

I believe it's a round trip voyage because we all start out loving ourselves. It's innate in us. Little boys and girls love themselves. From the time they can look in the mirror, they are captivated by their reflections and think they are the cat's meow. Then, as we age, we have experiences and become more critical of ourselves, and therein begins the journey away.

Most women I know — countless, precious, intelligent, capable women — have taken a one-way ticket away from self-love and towards self-criticism and shame. I don't want you to be one of them. I know only a handful of women that can genuinely and honestly say they love themselves entirely, who don't criticize themselves, and who appreciate themselves the way they are *and* the way they are not. To me, that is the final destination, where you arrive when you finally finish your return trip, whenever that may be.

I say "final destination" as if there is some ribbon of blue ticker tape waiting for you to bust through it, officially announcing the end of your race, but this isn't what I really mean. Each person's final destination is wherever that person needs to arrive – and that's different for every one of us. It could be that instead of reaching one point on a distant shore, you spend the rest of your time exploring one island, only to discover that it's not really an island at all, that it's more like an archipelago or peninsula, connected to others by underwater reefs or treetop canopies. Or, perhaps, some of us stay aboard our ships, discovering countless new ports and harbors to explore, because it seems they are limitless.

The point is, the journey of self-love begins the moment you are born, and each of us will have a certain time frame going away from ourselves, and a certain time frame coming back to ourselves. Sometimes these paths are a sprint away, and a slow, meander back. Other times they are like the paths of moths, flittering back and forth, coming back to the light whenever they find it, but wandering away just as easily. There are no right or wrong paths, timelines, or trajectories. There is only *yours*, and it's an adventure you will take, whether you want to or not, so I invite you to step into it.

Here I have to trust that the outcome of your journey will lead you to your life falling together, even if it feels like it has fallen apart countless times along the way. I wish that I could save you from all the heartache you will experience in your life, sweet girl. I wish I could feel it for you, but alas, I cannot. It would be like cutting open the chrysalis for a caterpillar slowly morphing into a butterfly: if you cut it open, the butterfly will not be strong enough to fly, because it is precisely by struggling *out* of the cocoon that it gains its strength. Know ahead of time that you *will* face hardships and obstacles. You will also make mistakes along the way. We are supposed to — it's alright, it's actually necessary, because that's how we learn and grow. There's nothing wrong with our lives when they get difficult.

That's one thing on my heart as I write you this book.

How I can care for my son is also in the forefront of my mind. I don't want him thinking I love him *less* because I wrote a book to you, my daughter... because it's for him, too. He has his own body issues, and will, as do most men I know (just ask your daddy and uncles). He will also love women in his life, whether they be partners, family, or friends, and I think it's important for him to have a glimpse of what they might experience living in their bodies.

The main reason I wrote this book to you, Athena, is because it didn't matter that I didn't love myself when I was the mother of a son. I thought I could fake it. But with you, another female, I knew I couldn't. You'd eventually see right through me.

I don't have firsthand experience as a male. I only have my own experience as a female, which doesn't even mean it will be yours, or any other woman's, for that matter. Although my experience is entirely unique to me, the feelings of inadequacy, shame, and self-criticism are familiar to most people, if not every single one of the 8 billion humans walking our planet. I don't know anyone, of any gender, who hasn't felt them at some point, or many, throughout their lives.

This book is a recollection of how I made the voyage away from myself, and then back to myself, after I had left pieces of myself behind, like a trail of crumbs. Thankfully, I was able to walk back through time and retrieve those crumbs, or at least most of them. This book is for YOU, my sweet girl, and it's also for any other woman, or any other human, who wants to come home again.

I don't pretend to have this all figured out. I'm still in this with you. I haven't arrived yet, but I know I'm on my way. Some days, the feeling of peace and joy is nearly overwhelming. Other days, it feels like I'm being pulled back out to sea by a rip current. I may never fully "arrive," but I will trust the process, and press on, because I know I have more to unlearn, more to explore, and more to love. You are worth it, sweet girl. And now I know another truth: I am worth it, too.

---

# PART ONE:

## Collision

*"Sometimes, when one person is missing,
the whole world feels depopulated."*
-Lamartine


"expect sadness
like
you expect rain.
both,
cleanse you."[3]
— Nayyirah Waheed

# Chapter 1

---

## Dad's Death

Dear Athena,

You'll discover, as you go through life, that there are moments in time where your existence is no longer the same. When one event changes your reality so drastically, that the timeline of your life is divided into a "before" and an "after" of that point. You'll likely have several of these occasions in your lifetime: they could be a marriage, births of children, deaths, divorces, jobs, or any number of momentous events, really.

For me, the singular moment that stands out as the most life-changing is July 4, 2009. To most people, that's American Independence Day. To me, it's the day my dad died.

He was in Bremerton, Washington, and I was in San Diego, California, visiting Kim & Pat. I had left my dog, Amos, with my dad, because neither one of them liked fireworks, and the two were going to hang out in the basement together, since it was cool, dark and quiet. My dad loved Amos, who I called a "NewFlatland Retriever," since he was a wonderful mix of Newfoundland and Flat-Coated Retriever. He was the reason my second dog, Hank, the first dog you knew, was also a Newfie mix. After spending time with Amos, my dad would occasionally comment, "What are you going to do when Amos is gone, Lis? He's the best dog ever."

My dad never asked me, "What are you going to do when I'm gone, Lis?" He never asked that question. Maybe because he thought he had more time. We all did.

While Kim, Pat and I were watching the local parade in Coronado, my dad mounted his bike for his last training ride in preparation for an upcoming bicycle trip he was about to take with my brother Chris through Glacier National Park. My brother Chris was camping in Leavenworth, Washington for the holiday, my brother Todd was in Mexico City, where he lived, and my mom (your MeeMa) was at home, with Amos, waiting for my dad to return.

It was a beautiful day in Kitsap County — the sky was bright blue and cloudless, it was warm and sunny, and the evergreen trees proudly lined the roads. My dad's route was long, winding past lakes, shops, and homes, mostly on back roads with wide shoulders. As he was on his way home, on a two-lane road with a 45mph speed limit, my dad was struck by a motorist making a left-hand turn.

The driver, who was driving with a suspended license, said my dad was hidden by a car going straight in the opposite direction, and since there were no other oncoming vehicles, she slowed down only as much as necessary to let the car pass, and then turned. And there was my father, in his colorful jersey, crossing the intersection into which she was turning.

She struck him, he was thrown 20 feet off his bike, and landed in the ditch beside the main road. Paramedics were called. They resuscitated him at the scene, and he was transported to Tacoma General Hospital, the nearest hospital able to deal with trauma.

I missed my mom's call, because, interestingly, I was visiting some of my dad's closest friends in Coronado, where he used to be stationed. I didn't see my mom's message until we got back to Kim and Pat's condo. When I pulled up her message, I heard her voice quaking with tears, explaining he had been struck. My knees buckled and I fell to the floor.

In shock, I called the hospital, and I remember being supremely grateful to have Kim, who is a nurse, by my side, so that she could translate their medical jargon into words I could understand: Multiple broken bones. Blood in brain. Not responsive. Outlook grim.

The next moments were a blur of calling Todd, my mom, packing up, booking my flight, and trying to contact Chris, who was out of cell range. One of his friends,

Stella, did one of the most selfless acts I will forever remember: she drove from her home in Seattle, all the way to Leavenworth, visiting each of the campgrounds until she found Chris to break him the news. And then, she got back in her car and followed Chris to Tacoma General to make sure his shellshocked body made it safely. Only then did she return to her own family. That's a good friend, baby girl.

My flight to Seattle had a stop in Los Angeles. After Kim and Pat dropped me off at the airport, I was distraught. I urgently needed to get there, but could go no faster than I already was. I saw an elderly Latina woman reading her Bible in Spanish, and I immediately approached her, begging her in Spanish to please pray for my dad, that he would live. Her answer, something about God's will, wasn't comforting.

I boarded the plane while talking with Todd, getting updates. Dad was still not responding, but his reflexes were good. The flight attendant requested I shut off the phone, which I, still crying, thought that was an impossibly unkind demand — didn't he know my phone was the only connection I had to my dad?

On the next flight, tears leaking continually from my eyes like a faucet barely left on, I was seated next to two Middle Eastern women wearing hijabs. Obviously concerned for their neighbor, they asked what was wrong, and tried to comfort me in my distress.

When we landed at Sea-Tac airport, I saw I had a message from Todd: "Lis, please call me before you talk to mom." Instantly, I knew something had changed. When I called, he told me that dad's brain had hemorrhaged, that his reflexes were gone, and he was now... brain dead. My dad, the champion of my life, was brain dead.

At that moment, a loud, desperate wail escaped my mouth as I fell to the ground, holding my head in my hands, rocking back and forth. I had the sensation of an out-of-body experience: I was above the scene, watching myself on the ground, as the baggage claim carousel steadily plodded along beside me, empty of any luggage.

Suddenly, two angels swooped down on either side of me and lifted me up. Bewildered, I looked up and saw it was the two women who had sat next to me on the plane. They walked me to baggage services and helped me through the necessary paperwork to retrieve my bag, which somehow hadn't arrived. Even though he was speaking plain English, I couldn't understand what the agent was saying to me. These ladies helped me, acting as intermediaries, and I am so grateful for their kindness. I've often wondered if they remember that distraught young woman they tried to soothe, and have asked for blessings over their lives multiple times.

My friend Wendy, who had driven all the way from Portland, Oregon to get me (I lived in Portland at the time), was waiting for me outside in the pick up/drop off lane. We headed to the hospital, and I became flustered when I couldn't find it. At a stop light, we noticed a police officer, so I rolled down my window and asked, "Where's Tacoma General Hospital?"

Seeing my face prompted him to ask, "What's the emergency?"

"My dad is dying!" I cried.

Flipping on his lights, he yelled, "Follow me!" and led the way. Another kindness shown for which I am grateful. We got there much faster thanks to his escort.

Upon reaching the hospital floor where my dad was being cared for, my eyes immediately sought him out. They scanned quickly past nurses, hesitating briefly on my mom and my cousin Brad, both somber and red-eyed. And then, my eyes found him. My hero, lying face up in bed, head completely bandaged, attached to tubes and machines keeping him alive.

Again that sob escaped me, and I ran to his side, willing him to wake up, begging him to open his eyes. I knew how much he loved us, so I thought, maybe, just *maybe,* it would be enough to pull him through. *"Please,"* I thought.

I gently grabbed his hand, I stroked it, I kissed it — and I wept, loudly. I cried so much that I remember being amazed by how many tears one body could produce in one day, for it seemed that mine had an endless supply. I couldn't stand the idea of being without my dad — never seeing his wide smile again, never hearing his voice, never feeling his bear hugs. I literally couldn't stand it; I was on my knees, and once I was assured I could not hurt him, I climbed gingerly onto the bed and snuggled on top of him. I held him, as much as I possibly could. I never wanted to let go, because when I did, I knew it would be the last time.

Eventually, Chris arrived, dazed and wounded. We spoke as a family, huddled together around the cell phone we used to include Todd the best we could, and remembered how my dad had specifically requested not to be kept alive if it required life support. Reluctantly, we complied with those wishes.

We each said our goodbyes, alone. Chris held the phone up to my dad's ear for Todd to say his. At Wendy's suggestion, we took one last treasured photo together as a family. And then, we pulled the plug.

Death did not happen instantly. The nurse had told us that muscle memory could keep his organs working for up to 24 hours longer. My dad was 69, and up until that day, in very good health. We all wondered how long it would take.

I thought the hardest part would be the waiting, but I was wrong. At first, his breathing stayed the same, but slowly, the pause between each breath grew longer. There were a few torturous, unexpected moments when my dad's body would lurch upward off the bed, noisily inhaling a big breath of air, gasping, and I thought, "Oh my God! It's a miracle! He's coming back to us!"

The first two times that happened, I really thought he was returning. Miserably, I realized, he was not. Those moments were sharp as knives in my heart, because they didn't mean he was coming back to us, only that his lungs were simply, and incredibly, doing their job, even as his body was shutting down.

My dad died at 6:24am on July 5, 2009.

The hardest part was not those clutching gasps of his body for air. It wasn't seeing the flat line on the heart monitor, although that did seem final. It wasn't going to the world's quietest breakfast at Denny's afterwards, either, where I watched the world go by outside as I was inwardly wondering, "How can they all keep going?  Don't they know my dad just died?"

The hardest part wasn't going home to my parents' house and seeing sweet Amos, who had been left alone for 18 hours (and still didn't have an accident, that amazing dog), and burying my face in his soft fur, hugging his big body for comfort.

It wasn't even the week that followed, when Kim, wonderful friend that she is, took off work and simply came to be with us, doing our laundry, our dishes, answering the door, and offering any other assistance we needed that first week of discombobulated grief.

No, the hardest part was walking into my dad's bedroom that first day back, and being overwhelmed with his scent, which I never even knew he had. Being able to smell him, but knowing that I would no longer see him, hear him, or touch him... at that moment, I knew he was gone. I fell forward onto his bed, inhaling his scent from his pillow as my body wracked with sobs.

My dad was gone. My greatest ally, cheerleader, and coach.

My mom was now a widow, after over 45 years together. My brothers were now without their role model. And me? I was my father's daughter; everyone always said so. Who was I if he was gone?

I would spend the next 10 years of my life figuring that out.

# Chapter 2

---

# The Gift Grief Gives

D ear Athena,

Many years ago, while I was teaching in Portland and before I had children, I read an article about a woman whose child had a life-threatening illness. In fact, the child had already lived past her life expectancy. The mother worked night shifts in order to be at home during the day, when it was more expensive to pay for the care her daughter required. She cared for her daughter during the day, after working all night, so she was constantly sleep deprived, and it was very hard on her health. It was exhausting work, emotionally and physically draining.

When asked during the interview how she continued given the conditions, and asked if she ever resented her situation, the mother responded (and I'm paraphrasing from memory): "Every day she is here is an extra gift. She was already supposed to be gone. She's not mine — I simply get the chance to care for her, so I take it."

Many times I've remembered that woman, especially on the days when I'm feeling exasperated as a mom. I've wondered if I could do the same if I had a similar situation. I'd like to imagine I would. I'm guessing most parents of a terminally ill child would do the same, but I suppose it also depends on if you frame it as an awful thing and wonder why it's happening to your child, or if you look at it as a chance to grow — an opportunity to be with someone you love and perhaps weren't meant to have for very long. While you don't want the illness, you understand the gift it is giving you: perspective.

Perspective that life is precious, that we are not promised tomorrow, that what makes life and living so priceless is the very impermanence of it, the realization that it can be taken away, at any moment. We won't be around all that long, in the grand scheme of things, even if we do live long lives. As poet Mary Oliver wrote, "Doesn't everything die at last, and too soon? Tell me, what is it you plan to do with your one wild and precious life."[4]

Your life is irreplaceable and invaluable, sweet girl. Grief offers us this gift of perspective. I was given this gift when my dad (your Big Pop) died. I was then, and continue to be, deeply sorrowful that he never got to be with you and Michael, that he never met Ben, that he wasn't at my wedding, or the births of my children. I am keenly aware and saddened by the fact that I was never able to call him with my concerns as I always thought I'd be able to do, and still want to do. There are countless memories I've wished for him to witness, endless moments I've wanted to share with him.

But I can't. He's not here.

What is here is *my* life, and the people in it. I got to have my dad for nearly 34 years of my life, which is longer than many people have their parents. And he was a "good" dad, too — acting as a surrogate father to many of my friends whose own fathers were not available or uninvolved in their lives.

Some people, understandably, might take the loss of someone so monumental, and interpret the fact that we only live once and to make every moment count as license to act recklessly, to drink alcohol excessively, to recreate with drugs, or engage in behaviors that put themselves or others at risk.

It's tempting to say, "Forget it! It's not worth it!" and let yourself run up credit card bills, eat the food that feels good in the moment (but makes you sick later), drink the wine, binge watch Netflix or YouTube instead of contributing to your day.

I understand the inclination. I've wanted to do that myself. In fact, I have, multiple times.

What I've come to realize, however, is that those behaviors, those activities done with a "screw it, I'm doing it" mentality — they're not really the life we want to be living. Most of the time, they're coping mechanisms or escape routes. They are ways to numb our pain, alleviate our anxiety, repress our resentment, or avoid our anger. They are signs that we have underlying issues that have been unresolved, unhealed, or at the very least, unaddressed.

Personally, I think this realization allows us to show ourselves grace, to understand our humanity. Of course we want to drown our sorrows. Of course we want to lighten the load. Of course we want to check out for a while. Who wouldn't want to do that? Emotions can be overwhelming, especially when there is pain and suffering involved.

They can be valuable, though, despite their heaviness, if we allow our grief, resentment, anger, anxiety, bitterness, or sadness to be present. If we really look at them as valid emotions, and wonder why we're experiencing them, then we can begin the process of healing, of humanizing ourselves, and of recognizing that there's nothing wrong with us at all.

Since becoming a mommy, I've often been gripped with the tremendous fear of losing you, or Michael, or your daddy. It's terrifying to think that every day there could be an accident, an illness, a perpetrator — anything — that could leave me living without you, any of you.

When I experience that fear, I no longer think of myself as a crazy woman, but as a normal mom who loves and adores her people, a woman who has built a sacred life she cherishes, and wants to see it continue.

Beauty doesn't exist without the knowledge that something can be ugly. Pain only exists because pleasure does, too. Joy comes from understanding sorrow. We can truly feel free only after we've felt the imprisonment of shame. Feeling loss means you once felt that you belonged. We can feast because we've seen famine. We love the light because we've experienced darkness. We can't appreciate one without the other. It's only through experiencing one that we understand the other — they are two sides of the same coin. You can't have one without the other. The most amazing part of this whole concept, though, is that once we've experienced loss, pain, ugliness, or shame, once you know how it feels, you can hold it within you, remembering, and choose to build up the other side. You can actively choose to cultivate freedom, joy, and beauty. You can choose to turn towards the light, love and belonging. You have the coin in your hand. You can choose which side of that coin faces up.

It's precisely *because* I have no idea how many days I will be given (gifted, really) to be with you and your brother that I am so conscious of my daily choices. It's why I eat nutritious foods, exercise regularly, prioritize my sleep, and continue learning and pushing myself. It's why I deal with the stress as well as I can, believing I'll figure out problems as I go, because as long as I'm alive, I have the chance to do so. I will pursue my absolute best life, my dreams, my health, and my family *because I can.* I do it because each day is a gift, and I'm giving each day my best. I hope you do, too.

Whenever you find yourself coping or numbing or avoiding your feelings, sweet girl, look for the feeling on the other side of that coin. It could be something you're wanting, but not getting. When you're in those moments, promise me you'll be brave enough to ask yourself WHY you are avoiding those feelings — and then, love yourself enough to explore the answers.

# Chapter 3

## Beauty from the Ashes

D ear Athena,

The other day as we were brushing our teeth together, I told you that I hoped we would always be friends, no matter what age you were. Confused, you answered, "Friends?"

I clarified, "You know, that we're able to talk about anything that happens in your life: fun stuff, disappointments, friendships, heartbreaks — because our hearts get broken many times."

"I know," you replied. "My heart's already been broken twice: when we gave away Lucy, and when Hank died. Well, three times. Not getting to meet your dad."

My heart squeezed when I heard that. Hank, your first furry friend, and Lucy, the first dog we got when we moved to Florida, were both pets you loved dearly. I knew it meant something to hear my dad lumped in among them. I love how deeply you feel, and how in tune you are with your emotions.

Something we discussed on our family road trip, though I'm not sure you remember, is the fact that fire can bring new growth. It adds nutrients to the soil that allow for new vegetation to sprout where once the land was barren.

The same thing happens in our lives, you know. When we gave away Lucy, the first dog we got after we lost Hank, we felt like we were letting her down; we felt a bit empty inside. But now, when we see her, it's clear how happy she is with her new sister Maggie. She's no longer anxious; she's safe. Her life *improved* because we were willing to let her go, even if we are still a little sad about it.

When Hank died, we were able to travel without missing him, and more importantly, without him missing us, which he would have done. Now, we remember his sweet nature, his soft, fluffy hair, his big block head, and insatiable desire to cuddle — and we are grateful for the time we got to have with him, because can you imagine never knowing Hank? What a bummer that would be. We have so many fun memories with him!

When my dad died, I actually felt like my heart was physically crushed, and I didn't know how I would go on, or even who I was anymore. I always imagined he would die *after* I had established a family of my own, once I'd figured out my life a little more. But he didn't.

In a way, his death was a catalyst for my rebirth —
having to discover who I was as myself, alone — not
as my father's daughter, or whoever else I thought I
had to be. I had to let go of someone I held dear in
order for me to also let go of who I thought I was
supposed to be, which was something I didn't even
know I needed to let go of at all. That was a long,
arduous, and often painful process, but worth the time
and effort.

You know, when people ask the question, "Who are
you?" and "What do you do?" I used to say things like,
"I'm Elisa", or "I'm a teacher," or "I'm a wife and mom."
Now I might just answer, "I'm a woman learning to
love myself in the midst of life." And that's because
I've learned to let go.

Two other things happened as a result of Big Pop's
death, and without those two things, three very precious people wouldn't be alive: you, your brother
Michael, and your cousin Mikey.

After my dad died, I couldn't go to the regular gym
anymore; it was too upsetting. It reminded me of him,
since he's the one that taught me to go and showed
me how to use the machines. Shortly after his death,
I tried CrossFit, where instead of using machines, you
learn functional movements that are constantly varied,
and performed at a high intensity. There are no mirrors,
only coaches and the class members. Long story short:

I loved it, and I stayed. Guess who I met there, about a year later? That's right: your dad.

Uncle Chris, who never took vacation time for the bike trip he was about to go on with Big Pop, ended up taking that vacation several months later, and going somewhere he had never been: Nicaragua. Guess who he met there, while he was touring the Somoto Canyon? That's right: Aunt Marvelliz and her family.

Without Big Pop dying, neither Chris nor I would've met our spouses, the parents of our children. Whether we would've met other partners, I can't say, but one fact I am sure of is that our current children wouldn't exist — and I can't imagine a world without you three in it.

Both Michael and Mikey are named after your Big Pop. I suppose that's a testament to how much he meant to both of us (of course he was special to Uncle Todd, too, but his girls had already been born and named).

I continue to be heartbroken when I think about how your Big Pop, a pediatrician and lover of children, never got to meet you, or Michael, or Mikey. He would have absolutely delighted in you. I feel my heart constrict when I let myself miss him, when I think about him, with his grandkids.

Michael and Mikey got his name. What did you get from him? I believe you got a visit.

When I was one month shy of your due date, I was missing my dad tremendously. It was high summer, and I was remembering how beautiful my dad's summer garden always was, with the happy hostas, the gladiolus, the Shasta daisies, and his favorite, dahlias, of all colors, shapes and sizes. He took great care to dig up his dahlia tubers every winter, and store them in the garage until next spring.

We had moved into our new house (the "Happy House") a few months before, so it was our first summer there, and we didn't know what would come up from the flower beds. While I was weeding one day, I noticed a sprout that looked an awful lot like a dahlia sprout – so I let it grow to see what it would become.

As it grew, it was obviously a dahlia: it had a tall, strong stem, dark green leaves, and buds that looked exactly like what I had seen in my dad's garden, and what he had helped me plant in my first home in Beaverton. The only question was, what kind of dahlia would it be? Dinner plate? Pom pom? Size? Color?

On August 24 (your Uncle Todd's birthday), six days before you arrived, the blossom opened, in my absolute favorite color: the orange pink peach of sunrise.

This not only squeezed my heart, but a few tears from my eye along with it. I looked skyward, a lump in my throat. I was so grateful, because it was clearly your Big Pop telling me he was there, that he was watching, present to the miracle of your birth. A dahlia, that I had not planted, in the color of sunrise, which was the time of day both he and I held sacred and silent.

Beauty can come from the ashes, baby girl. It happens, but you must look for it.

---

# PART TWO:

## False Foundation

*"The man who does not value himself,*
*cannot value anything or anyone."*
-Oscar Wilde

*"Whatever we plant in our minds and nourish with repeti-*
*tion and emotion will one day become a reality."*
-Earl Nightingale

# Chapter 4

## You Don't Matter

D ear Athena,

Several years ago when I was going through some personal growth work with the company Landmark Worldwide, we identified instances in our lives that had created stories in our minds, stories that then began to run the show. The fact that we have these moments and stories doesn't mean that anything is wrong with us, by the way. It merely shows that we are human, because this is how our human minds operate.

Love and belonging are essential for every human on earth, no matter what. It's part of our survival that we belong. That's one of the reasons we fear rejection so powerfully. Of *course* we worry about being left out — our ancestors would most likely have died if they were, so it makes sense. We are hard-wired to want to be part of a tribe. So, when we experience events that threaten us psychologically; meaning, they trigger a fear related to belonging or being loved, it causes a stress response in our bodies: the fight, flight or freeze mode. Another aspect of that response is our minds trying to make sense of them, cataloging these events in case we need to draw from this experience in the future. Our brains assign a story to the threat, so that we can organize the event in our mind and learn from it, thereby avoiding future threats and survive. At least, that's the idea. Of course, when we are children, we lack the experience, knowledge, and critical thinking to know whether these events are actual threats or only perceived threats. Much of the time, what we *make* them mean is not actually *what* they mean, but it's what our young brains think we need to survive, so that's the meaning our minds have given them.

The overarching theme of the events I identified was that I — my voice, my opinion, my personhood — don't matter. I carried that false truth with me for a very long time, and if I'm honest, still do. I have a very hard time believing that anything I could say would benefit anyone, and it makes me sad that anyone would think this, let alone myself. Which is one of the reasons I make myself do things like host a podcast, post on social media, and even write this book. It requires courage for me to do all of those things, because with each word I speak out loud or in print, I'm going against the message that was ingrained in my head for so long, and both my body and mind resist it.

When you read my stories, you might wonder why I made them be such big deals, because they aren't very significant in the grand scheme of things. But they were a big deal to me as a child, and I took them all as evidence that I wasn't important enough to have an opinion that mattered, or had anything worthwhile to say. They probably *didn't* mean what I made them mean, but that's the thing — it doesn't matter what event it is, or what actually happens — it's what *we* make it mean in our minds that ends up affecting us.

*You* have probably already experienced a few things that you've made mean something, and it's important to know we all do this "story making," so that you can be on the lookout for when you are making up stories in your head, or focusing on what actually happened.

For example, a few nights ago, Michael didn't want to go to bed yet, and rather than fight with him, we said, "Ok, stay up. No screens or games, but you can read." For some reason, your dad said *you* had to go to bed, which was surprising, since your daddy usually lets you do what Michael is doing. It was also a little tricky because you share a room. Michael had a flashlight under his comforter he was using to read.

The next morning, you were tired because you said Michael kept you from sleeping, and then you complained, "You *always* let Michael do *everything*, and you never let *ME* do *anything*!" This is an example of how you could interpret that one night as meaning that we don't give you freedom or choice, and continue finding examples of that as you grow older.

Would you like to read a few examples of story making from my life, to see what I mean?

When I was five, we lived in Rota, Spain. I went to a Spanish kindergarten, and we lived on a cul-de-sac where there were some other kids — a few were my brothers' ages, and two were my age. I'll call them George and Helen. We tended to play together a lot, and one of the games we played was "Castle," where there was a king, queen, and servant. Naturally, George's role as "king" went uncontested — he got to be king every time. There were two of us left as options to be "queen" and "servant." You might think we took turns, but somehow, my request to be queen consistently went denied. I don't remember if I never spoke it, or if it was ignored... it just never happened, and I was always the servant. As a result, I was left feeling unimportant, and unworthy to be the queen. Did they mean for that to happen? Probably not. Most likely, they just wanted to play and be king and queen. My five year old mind made up the false truth that I was unimportant.

Another incident, also in Spain, was on one of our many camping trips through Europe in Harvey, our blue pop-up-top VW camper. I loved those trips because they were always an adventure, with dad driving and mom navigating in the passenger seat, holding one of those giant paper maps, unfolded across her lap. I have many memories of those maps flapping in the wind, windows rolled down, green grassy pastures and hills rolling by, and even some purple cows. My favorite place to sleep was in the pop-up-top section itself – I fit perfectly there and that made me feel really special.

One day, we were all loaded up in Harvey, going some-where: mom, dad, Todd, Chris and me. Suddenly, the engine caught fire and there were flames coming out of the front! Dad quickly pulled over and everyone hurried out of the car and turned to look at it, wondering what to do. I know this, because I saw all their faces through the windshield, because I was still *in* the car, buckled in my carseat, unable to get out. Finally, my mom realized I was still inside, and, panicking, she went the long way around the van to get me out. I took that to mean I was the least important person, that I didn't matter much. Did my mother say I was the least important child? Of course not! As a mom, I'm sure she was frantic that her only daughter was trapped in the car, felt miserable for leaving me in there, and just wanted to get me out! I was the one who made up that story in my mind, and let it sit there, festering.

A few years later, I was an eager student in elementary school. I suppose I've always loved learning, much like you and Michael do. Like many enthusiastic students, when the teacher asked a question to the class, I raised my hand to answer, and I did this often. At one point, a teacher told me to put my hand down, and let other kids answer. As a teacher later in life, I know that was not an ill-intentioned comment; it was an attempt by the teacher to encourage more participation from other kids. But, to my child's heart, it was telling me that my input didn't matter. She didn't want to hear what I had to say.

Also in grade school, during PE, I was always picked last for teams. I absolutely hated the feeling of standing there, face burning, watching every other kid get chosen before I did. Every other selection was another vote for my presence not being important — in fact, being a detriment. No one wanted me on their team. I sucked. I was the opposite of an asset; I was a burden. The message I received loud and clear was: I brought the team down. So, guess who didn't play team sports? That's right, your mom. Is it any wonder, though?

I reluctantly played basketball my freshman year at my dad's urging, and I tried volleyball as a junior because my friend Tawnya asked me to do it with her. My efforts were less than my best, although they weren't my worst, and I stuck out those seasons, never to play again.

I didn't even consider myself athletic until years later, after I joined CrossFit, although I did go the gym and dabble in classes like spinning and boxing. Note that both of those are individual sports. That message I got

as a kid was strongly embedded, and I'm not too proud
to say that is one reason I still don't play sports — I fear
it will be true.

My first year of high school, we had moved to a new
place: Coronado, California, a beach town in San Diego.
I was thirteen years old, and I knew no one. Typically,
students in Coronado schools were either insiders who
grew up there, or outsiders who were Navy kids, like me.
Thankfully, I met a few other newcomers, and one local
who would end up being one of my closest friends in life:
Kim.

But then, they all got boyfriends, and became sexually
active. Most of them also started drinking alcohol, and
when I didn't, I got left behind. I didn't have a boyfriend,
so I couldn't do *that*, but I could drink, so this soon led to
me drinking during open lunch, and returning to science
class buzzed. I really liked that class, too, and the teacher.
I drank on weekends, and had several blackout moments
I don't remember. I'd wake up in places I didn't remember
going, notice things like rings missing off my fingers, and
once, some of my hair had been cut. I didn't like drinking,
honestly — but I simply *knew* that if I didn't participate,
I would be left alone. Ironically, even while engaging in
that behavior, I felt lonelier than ever.

I had vivid nightmares of being abandoned on giant
sand dunes, and made tearful phone calls to my friends
in Washington state. My dad overheard one of them with

my friend Heather, which led to him requesting a transfer back to Washington so we could return there — which was a big deal. My dad felt like he could actually settle in San Diego, possibly even retire there. He cared about *my* well-being so much that he was willing to leave a post he truly loved, just for me. I wish I understood that sacrifice back then, but I didn't; I was too wrapped up in my own stories and beliefs to notice.

My dad *did* apply for that transfer, but since it would take about six months for him to get it, he arranged for me to live with Heather's family for a while until he could get a condo situated for his mom (my grandma and both of our namesakes, Mum Jane) and me to live in until they could return. I really loved that time with her. She was steady as a rock in her faith, in her love for me, and in her routine. We made our meals on the stove, without the microwave, and she taught me to drive. I remember one of my friends remarking that I drove like a grandma, and I felt very proud. She had been a teacher of the deaf and blind, and they named the library of her old church in Florida in her honor — and the fact that she cared about me — well, let's just say her presence was a balm of reassurance.

That time with her was a very special experience for me, and I'd imagine, for her also. I don't remember feeling so consumed with negative thoughts when I lived with her, either. This could be due to the fact that it was a novel situation, my sense of security with her, or both. Once our six months were over and my dad was stationed back in Bremerton, Mum returned to Florida and I moved back in with my parents.

I wish I could say those negative beliefs went away once I was back with my Washington friends, but they didn't. I was convinced that as long as I kept at it, as long as I played the part I was "supposed" to play in each setting — whether that be with friends, classmates, teachers, parents, or boyfriends — it would all be fine. I would fit in. Who I was didn't matter, anyway. All those instances I experienced as I was growing up had taught me that. At least, that's what I believed at the time. It was clear I didn't matter — and even though it wasn't true, I thought it was, so it became true. I found evidence to support it, wherever I went.

I share my stories as examples of how masterful our minds are in making meaning out of our experiences, regardless of our background or who we are. They also show how common it is, and often tragic, for us to live by those misinterpretations, those made-up meanings, which are often simple misunderstandings.

Another word for all of these stories is "drama." We create the drama in our lives, sweet girl. I didn't know I was making it all up in my head. It seemed so real! And it will to you, too. It's only by examining your head junk head-on that you can learn to expose and debunk the lies. It may not be fun, but it's the best way to keep you out of victim mode, Athena, and I know you are strong enough to do it.

# Chapter 5

---

# Worthless

D ear Athena,
   It's not hard to pinpoint exactly when I began feeling like a worthless human being — a person who had no value. As I mentioned, I had moments growing up where I felt left out, overlooked, and abandoned. I'm guessing that almost every child in the United States, and many other parts of the world, has had moments like that, too. So, while I can't say they were definitive, they were impactful, because my brain was still immature and made all those instances mean I must be less than other people. I created stories around those moments, like "I am unlovable." "I am easy to overlook." "I'm not important." We all do this, and then we find evidence for these stories, and we create self-fulfilling prophecies that add more fuel to the fire of our self-doubt and insecurity.

   If I'm honest, though, and extremely vulnerable, I'll tell you when I lost any shred of remaining self-respect. It was in 1992, when I lost my virginity at age 16, during my junior year of high school. More specifically, it was a few months *after* that day.

I was the last one of my friends to have sex, or at least that I knew at the time. I felt old then, but when I look back at myself now, I was so young and tender, like a fresh shoot coming up from the ground, fragile and easily trampled. I felt I had already been left behind by friends in San Diego for not being sexually active, so when my friends in Washington began having sex, I worried that history would repeat itself.

That spring, a popular senior athlete showed interest in me. I didn't know him well; I didn't even know that much about him, but I knew he was good looking, fit, and popular. I'm guessing we hung out a few times, but I don't really remember if we did. All I remember is the day he came over after school while my parents were gone, and we had sex on the daybed downstairs. The next day was nothing special. We may have even briefly "dated," and a few weeks after that, there was a dance. He went with his ex-girlfriend, where they rekindled their on-again, off-again relationship. It almost felt like it never happened.

Except.

A month or so later, while bathing, I felt a bump on my vagina, and I knew something was awry. I felt around and noticed a few more. Since I had been taught that having sex before marriage was "wrong," I kept my mouth shut about it. Embarrassed by what it could mean, I didn't tell any friends, and looked up a local health clinic in the phone book. (This was in the days before the Internet. Since you don't know what phone books are, I'll tell you: They were giant paperback books the size of your school binder, a thousand pages long, heavy as bricks, and filled with names of businesses, listed alphabetically, and their phone numbers. You used your fingers and eyes to find the numbers.  One phone book was the White Pages, which had families' and people's names and numbers; the others were the Yellow Pages, with the businesses, listed alphabetically.  Ours were stacked underneath the fruit basket in our kitchen.) I called and made myself an appointment.

I had to skip school to be there, so I forged a note saying I had an orthodontist appointment, and secretly drove myself to the clinic in Charlie, our old blue Volvo.

I was scared, truth be told. It felt cold, impersonal, and unkind. Sterile and unfeeling. When the clinician finished her exam, she stated bluntly, "You have HPV. Do you know what that is?"

When I said no, she explained it, but all I heard was the word "lifelong," meaning that I would have it forever; it would never go away.

So that you have some context, HPV stands for Human Papillomavirus, also called venereal warts.  It's a very common sexually transmitted infection (STI). In those days, it was called a disease, and it was thought to be permanent. You could spread the virus to other people, even after having the venereal warts removed. (Conversely, another common STI is genital herpes, which can come and go, and you spread it only when you have the physical symptoms of it.)

When she informed me of my condition, immediately my heart constricted. I burned with shame as I drove home, the voices inside my head speaking loudly, and with certainty: "Ooooh, Elisa. You are *dirty*. You are *disgusting*. You are *worthless*. How could you be so stupid? Who would ever want you now?" All I ever had to offer was my body, and now, that was damaged goods. It was defective — even repulsive.

I knew my parents would be so disappointed in their little girl. There was no *way* they would see me the same way. To consider they would still love me, be proud of me, or think highly of me was impossible. I could never measure up to their ideal again.

Alone I dealt with the warts, getting them frozen off, because I was too disgusted with myself to tell anyone. Eventually I did, though I can't tell you when it was. I somehow told my mom, too, and once she knew, I started having regular gynecologist appointments, and getting biopsies when I had an abnormal Pap smear, since HPV increased the risk of cervical cancer.

When I learned I had HPV after my very first sexual encounter, I left my self-respect behind at that health clinic. I began barricading myself away from my parents, and giving it the meaning that I was no good, that I was flawed and broken. I thought there was something wrong with me, and no one would love me. I actually believed this, and so I acted like it. I didn't respect my body — after all, it was spoiled.

Then, my senior year of high school, one year later — I was voted "best body," which was exactly what was *not* best for my body — or my mind. Was this some cruel joke? Didn't they know I was rotten inside? Apparently, it wasn't. I was the female vote, my friend Ron was the male vote, and we had our picture taken and printed in the yearbook's "Hall of Fame" pages.

Since this vote came after my exposure to HPV, I burned with shame inside. I was one year younger than everyone else (due to starting school in Spain), and I still felt like I didn't really belong after having moved away and back in the middle of high school. I had already compromised my body for the sake of "being popular" and having friends, and look where that had landed me.

Plus, I absolutely hated that while I apparently fit the description of what society said was "pretty," to me that was obviously a farce. I couldn't have articulated this at that time, but I knew even then that what the media portrayed as pretty mattered more than anything else, and I hated it. I wanted to believe I had something else to offer besides my body, which was now a cracked facade, but what could it be? The sense that I was being played like a puppet in some game was creepy — but I didn't know there were other options.

The shame and loneliness that simmered beneath the surface was hidden by my mask of an achieving student, but those insecurities were the basis for all my decisions. I felt rotten inside, like those Hogwarts jelly beans — they look delicious on the outside, but actually taste like vomit, or ear wax.

That high school vote confirmed what I had suspected all along: I was only liked because of my body. I was also hated for my body. People can be very mean to each other when we're all vying for what we think is acceptance; when we're all trying to "win" at someone else's game. It fosters cruel "us vs. them" mentalities.

Either way, it seemed clear that my body was all I was good for. That picture, published in the yearbook? It solidified the message as I went off to college: "Your body, Elisa. It's what people notice about you, and it's the reason you matter."

That vote was another piece of evidence against my defense as a person of value; it was an exhibit for the prosecution that I was only worthwhile if I did something remarkable, or produced something others deemed worthwhile. Bottom line: I was only as good as I reflected *other* peoples' standards, and this belief stayed with me long into adulthood.

What were *my* standards? I had no idea. I didn't even know I could have my own standards. Me? What did *I* want? What did I value? What did I deem important? I couldn't tell you, because it was never considered. It didn't matter anyway, because even if I had taken the time to reflect, I wouldn't have had the courage to communicate it. That would've been too big a risk for my young, insecure heart.

Knowing I had a higher risk of cervical cancer, knowing that I would have to tell every single guy I was interested in that I had HPV — and would have it forever  — was devastating, and far beyond the level of vulnerability I was prepared to share. Telling a sexual partner would mean *they* would decide if I was worth the risk of "contamination." Having to disclose this confidential information made me relive the feeling of being used, dirty, and infected every time. I wholly hated myself for it.

But I did tell them. I told my boyfriend my senior year of high school, the guys I dated in college, the men afterwards as a single adult. And every time, I was reminded of how disgusting I was.

Some of the men did choose me. Some did not. Because I didn't respect myself, other people — especially men — didn't respect me, either. It's hard to care for and respect someone who doesn't care what happens to her.

Many of the men I dated were unfaithful and cheated on me with other women; one even paid to cheat on me with a prostitute. (By the way, I am not judging that woman — not anymore. Now I understand she was on her own voyage, and I imagine she had her own stories she was working through — as did those men who lied and cheated.)

Of course I was offended, but there was a part of me that excused their behavior: "Well, I am damaged goods, after all. I guess I'm not good enough to keep." I didn't think I was worthy of real love, so I chose (unconsciously, of course) guys who would treat me not unkindly, but without any real regard. I was there for them to use as they wished, and that's about it.

It's difficult to write those sentences, because it's hard to admit I was that girl. However, I also have empathy for her, because she was simply doing what she thought she needed to do in order to be loved and accepted, given that she had deemed herself unlovable. As a result, she felt worthless and lonely for a very long time, from the young age of 16 until she was in her mid thirties. She - I - was unfulfilled in my relationships for decades, wondering if this was all there was. It didn't seem all that great.

Not all the men I dated were unfaithful. Several accepted me for me, and loved me in their own ways. One was far away and we were too young, one couldn't handle my history, one was mismatched. And one was your dad, who was the real keeper.

One year at my annual check up, right around the time I had begun seriously dating your dad, my doctor told me I had no signs of HPV. These days, we know it's the most common sexually transmitted infection, but when I contracted it, it was considered a permanent disease. I was beyond excited about this news, but also incredulous. My body had likely overcome the virus several years before, but when you've spent 20 years of your life believing the worst about yourself, it's hard to break free and consider a new alternative.

Writing about this now, so many decades later, I feel supremely grateful to have revisited my younger self, to view her through a lens of love and compassion. She really *was* something, so strong and brave. I feel like we've restored my worth together. We've pieced together my wholeness. Would I change it if I could go back? Probably. But isn't that somewhat of a useless question? What happened, happened — and I am who I am today because of all of it, and everything that ensued afterwards. What's important is that not only have I stopped giving *away* my value, I *took it back*. My value was far more than a small infection of my body. I was not that infection. I was not even my body. I was, and am, *me*.

As you have relationships, sweet girl, inevitably you will get hurt. You will be tempted to make rejection mean something about yourself, when in reality, it re-veals something about both of you. In every single re-lationship, both parties are learning. When you grow up and begin dating, of course there will be failures. You're both figuring out what works for you, and what doesn't. This is to be expected. Trial and error is one of the best teachers. There's no rush to get it right, or find the right person. (It took me 36 years to find mine.) In relationships, both people are learning how to be in communication, how to set boundaries, to give and take, compromise and collaborate. There will be high and low moments in every single one, I'm guessing. And each one will give you another opportunity to stay true to your *self* - to keep it, grow it, and care for it. Your *self* matters, baby girl, even in, *especially* in, a relationship.

# Chapter 6

## Freshman Fifteen

Dear Athena,

I'll never forget the day I came home from college for winter break my freshman year. I was so excited to be home! My older brothers, who are 7 and 10 years older than me, were both going to be there, and we all loved our family Christmas traditions: Christmas cookies, pajamas, family pictures, wearing our Christmas-themed suspenders and socks, opening gifts one by one, from youngest to oldest, playing games like Uno and Charades, and of course all the food: aebelskivers, beignets, and rolls & gravy for breakfasts, Mum's rolls with prime rib and turkey for dinner, chocolate pie and Christmas cookies for dessert. But the very best part? That was being together.

Back in those days, traffic from Portland to Bremerton was lighter, so my drives were usually right around two hours and 45 minutes. I drove home, parked my light blue Mazda 626 (my friend Dan called it the "Mazdarati"), and walked in the kitchen door. To my surprise and delight, my oldest brother Todd was in the kitchen, having already arrived.

He turned, looked at me, and the first words I remember him saying were, "Dang, Lis! You've put on some *weight!*"

And I had! One reason why was cereal.

In high school, I was allowed to have cereal for breakfast. No sugar cereal, mind you — it was either plain Cheerios, Special K, or GrapeNuts. I could sprinkle my own sugar on that cereal, but we NEVER got boxed sugar cereals. EVER.

My first day in college, I walked into the Bon Appetit, our cafeteria, walked through the hot food section and chose my meal. I went to a table, ate my food, and then dutifully began walking to the back of the building to deposit my tray on the conveyor belt to be sanitized. As I carried my tray of empty dishes through the threshold of the back room, I stopped abruptly.

The heavens opened up, sunlight started streaming down in front of me, and I swear I heard a chorus of angels singing. Directly in front of me was an entire *wall* of *barrels* filled with cereals of all kinds. We're talking Honeycomb, Life, and Captain Crunch. Froot Loops, Golden Grahams, and Applejacks. Cinnamon Toast Crunch, Cocoa Puffs, and Lucky Charms! Turns out they we*re* magically delicious!

From that day forward, I had cereal as part of every single meal of the day, and I'm pretty sure I tried them all. (Little did I know that my cereal habit was a huge contributing factor to my poor health! It'd be over a decade later when I learned that those cereals are a main culprit in chronic disease, partly due to their stimulation of insulin production in your body.)

Anyway, back to my interaction with Uncle Todd.

I have no recollection of what I said in response to his comment. I probably shrugged and laughed it off, we hugged, and started catching up. Your uncle Todd is witty, and he loves to crack jokes. (In fact, he doesn't remember this incident, and when I reminded him about it, he admitted he is the last person who should be mentioning someone else's weight, since he's had his own ups and downs with the scale.) I knew in my mind that he wasn't passing a value judgment on me as a person, he was simply stating a fact. I *had* put on weight, and he was surprised by it. I equate his statement to many I would later hear when I lived in Mexico, where they nicknamed people "Gordo" (fatty), "Flaco" (skinny), or "Calvo" (baldy). They were just calling it like it is, not meaning any harm in it — in fact, they were often terms of endearment.

Even though I knew this in my logical mind, his statement triggered that shame inside me. He didn't make me feel terrible, *I* did. I made up that story. I took it as yet another indicator that my body shape dictated my value

— and having a bigger body shape apparently deval-
ued me. It was evident that I needed to switch things
up, or I wasn't going to be worth anything.

All through college, and beyond, I thought about
food as directly related to how I looked, and how much
I weighed. Weight was my goal, instead of how I felt, or
performed, or how healthy I actually was (or wasn't).
Food was not viewed as nutrition, it was a formula,
and I was trying to figure it out.

As a college student, my budget and priorities
meant Pasta Roni boxes, Ramen, and 99-cent bean
burritos from Taco Bell, with three packets of hot
sauce each. And alcohol, of course. Did I eat vegetables? I don't remember, honestly. Did I take diet
pills to keep me thin, regardless of the side effects?
Yes. Did I love the big boobs that came with the birth
control pills I was on? Absolutely! It helped me get
closer to that image the media kept presenting of
what I was supposed to look like. Did I consider what
my lack of nutrition and lifestyle were doing to my
metabolic function, my energy, or my emotional and
mental health? Not a chance. It wasn't even on my
radar.

All that mattered was keeping the curves — but not
too much of them. Oh, and keeping my grades at a place
where my parents wouldn't question, which wasn't too
hard for me, because I loved learning and enjoyed nearly

all my classes (except that one Economics class, though; that was rough!).

I treated my body like a separate entity. I wasn't my own partner. I got angry at my body when it wouldn't do what I wanted it to, even though it was literally doing the best it could. I didn't nourish my body; I starved and neglected it, giving it almost no fresh foods and almost everything processed.

It was uncomfortable feeling unworthy, feeling like I wasn't enough, and very alone. As a result, I numbed my discomfort with a lot of alcohol, mostly hard liquor at the time, because that was before I developed a taste for wine and beer. I was saturating my blood with alcohol every weekend, regularly smoking marijuana, and thinking I was fine. I wasn't fine, but somehow, I thought I would be.

My coping mechanism, my way of distracting myself from my discomfort and shame, was drinking, mainly. There are many ways people distract themselves, though: shopping, binge watching TV, vaping, scrolling on social media, staying busy, sarcasm, eating, sex, pornography, avoidance, and many, many more. Most of us will use several throughout our lives. It's especially easy to pick up these coping mechanisms and distractions from our friends. Not only do we like hanging out with them, but we also often feel intense pressure to do what they do, or we won't belong anymore. Watch out for yours, okay, sweet girl?

Let me remind you, right here and right now: your body size does not diminish your value. It does not enhance your value, either. Your body keeps showing up for you, every dang day, so that you can live your life. Be on the lookout for coping mechanisms that are covering up an uncomfortable feeling you'd rather not experience. Take caution when you feel pressure to do something that all your friends are doing, whether this be pressure they put on you, or you put on yourself. Chances are, they're feeling the same way and don't want to admit it. Let yourself feel the discomfort instead of hiding it, and see what's underneath. Recognize the lies that are trying to tell you that you need to look a certain way, or act a certain way, to be accepted, because that's what they are: lies that will keep you playing small, shriveling up inside while you waste the days away. Even if those lies are loud inside your head, remember this: their volume doesn't mean they are true or valid.

Your body is your vessel on this path of life, Athena. It can only work with what you give it. You are made for living, so give your body the best you can offer, instead of the leftovers.

# Chapter 7

---

# Self-Fulfilling Prophecies

Dear Athena,

Last night was Halloween, and we joined your friend's neighborhood, like we did last year. Last year, after about four houses, you told me you felt sick, and wanted to go home. As soon as we got home, you puked, and kept puking for hours, staying home from school the next day. This year — no puking! Hooray! You did, however, fall and scrape your knee. When we were brushing our teeth at the end of the night, you declared, "Next year, I'm not going trick or treating. I'm cursed!"

I share this because it's a great example of how quickly one — or in this instance, two — events can be made into a story, given significance, and impact the rest of our lives, creating self-fulfilling prophecies of doom. I've done it myself, very well, as you've seen from the chapters of this book so far.

After my dad died, I was forced to look at who I was, to consider my life and what I was doing with it. I tentatively started to build a life for myself. Through CrossFit, I gained physical and mental fortitude. Through writing, I found emotional healing. By owning my own home, I found independence. I ventured out and tried new paths.

I began to trust myself again, to believe I was competent, that I could handle what came my way. I studied myself through the Enneagram and other personality tests and started looking at myself objectively, and began to treat myself nicely, choosing more nourishing foods and taking better care of myself. I started setting boundaries — small ones. I began to believe that maybe I *was* worth love, and that I *did* have something to offer — not only as a teacher, but as a human being and a partner.

That began a new self-fulfilling prophecy, one where I set standards for myself, as well as for being in a relationship. It took me a while to get proficient at those new standards, to regularly implement them, but I got there — and now, they are second nature to me. I don't even think about them, just like I didn't think about my old damaging beliefs; I just assumed they were true.

Please hear this, baby girl: all of your beliefs — especially the negative ones you say about yourself, need to be questioned. This series of questions I learned and adapted from Byron Katie is very practical.[5]

When you are believing something about yourself, ask these questions:

1. Is it true?

2. What is the evidence it is true?

3. Has there ever been a time in your life when this was not true?

4. What is an alternate truth?

5. Does this belief serve you?

Let's take a look at your Halloween curse using these questions.

1. Is it true?  No, you are not cursed. No one cursed you for all time on Halloween.

2. What is the evidence it is true?  You had two Halloweens, back to back, where you went to the same neighborhood. The first time you ended up vomiting, the second time, you fell and scraped your knee.

3. Has there ever been a time in your life when this was not true?  Yes. You've spent other Halloweens — in Italy, with your cousins in Oregon, and with your brother — all without any mishaps.

4. What is an alternate truth?  Perhaps you had caught a tummy bug earlier in school, and it caught up with you that night. Maybe you were

having such a great time with friends, enthusiastically running from house to house, and you
tripped on something, then you fell. You continued on, gathering an exorbitant amount of candy
you still haven't finished eating, months later.

5. Does this belief serve you? Not really. All it
   will do is cause you to anticipate "bad things"
   happening on Halloween, and take away from
   the fun of it.

I realize this is a silly example. Even still, it demonstrates that, regardless of the severity of the belief that's
running through your mind, these questions can help you
identify false beliefs, the ones that will keep you stuck,
or even pull you back.

I didn't have these questions when I learned I had
HPV and thought I was worthless. If I had, I could have
completed this exercise. I might have seen that it *wasn't*
true, that I *did* have worth: I had friends who cared about
me and enjoyed being with me, I had a sharp brain that
sought knowledge, I had deep compassion for others. My
only evidence that I was worthless was an infection I had
in my body, one that I could spread to other people if I
wasn't careful. I hadn't always thought I was worthless,
like when I was young and carefree, when I aced my
classes and was learning, and when I was with family.
An alternative truth I could have considered might have

been that it was a gift to me, to allow me to sift out the people who really valued me for my intellect, my personality, my love, instead of merely for my body. Did the belief that I was worthless serve me? No. On the contrary, it nearly destroyed me.

To thrive, sweet girl, to embody your power, you must choose the beliefs that serve you, that grow you, and that move you forward, because they will become your automatic pilot. If you don't, your automatic pilot will be programmed for you by your reactions, instead of your intentions, and you have no idea where you'll end up. So be powerful: question, reflect, and choose.

# Chapter 8

---

# Shaping Self-Awareness

D ear Athena,
  You might think, based on how I'm talking about how I didn't love myself most of my life, that I grew up in an unloving household. Why else would I be so critical of myself, or dislike myself so much? Actually, a better word may be that I *disregarded* myself — I did not regard myself as a person worth considering, so I simply didn't.

But I *didn't* grow up in an unloving household. On the contrary, I was very loved, and I knew it. I knew the story of my existence; the family story goes like this: after two boys, my dad wanted a girl, and he would keep trying until he got one. I knew I was wanted, I knew I mattered to them. I also believed, that even though my brothers aggravated me (like Michael does you), they loved me. I admired the heck out of them, and treasured every moment I got with them. Once they left for college when I was in 7<sup>th</sup> grade, I looked forward to holidays even more, because I knew I'd get to see them. Even today, any visit with them is special.

So where did my low self-worth come from? I suppose the answer is from my immature mind trying to make sense of the world around me. Our brains don't fully mature in their ability to function until we are in our *late* twenties, and by then, most of us are living on our own, or away from our parents or other formative figures — at least that is typical here in the United States.

When things would happen, things that now, as a mature adult with life experience, I can see were not very consequential, or weren't meant to be negative (like being picked last, or a teacher asking me to give other kids a turn to speak, or my friends choosing to do other things than hang out with me), my developing mind and my emotions would make up the stories that those things meant I was defective, there was something wrong with me, I was not good enough as I was.

And I continued with that interpretation of events each time something else similar happened, until it became a belief pattern, running in the back of my mind, like computer programming. It was my default way of being in the world — I existed, but I wasn't worth much. I was here, but I was worth only what I could produce.

When I was in middle and high school, I showed my report card to my parents each grading period. I remember my dad saying, "You don't have a job right now that pays money. Your job is school, and your job is to get good grades." Even though I *knew* my dad adored me, I interpreted that as if he had said, "Lis, you will be disappointing me if you get anything less than As and possibly a few Bs. Anything less than that is unacceptable." I believed that I would be letting him down, that he would love me less, if I didn't get straight As. He never said that to me, and as a parent I'm confident he would never love me *less* if I got bad grades. But I believed it, and undoubtedly thought it was true.

I've since understood that this is a common tendency; it happens to all of us. We all make up stories in our heads about the things we experience, and those stories become messages to our brains, which later become the filters we use to view the world. Or, our blueprints for working with people, as Dr. Joan Rosenberg calls them.[6] It happens young, too. Experts say that by the age of 13 or 14, or even younger, we have all established a certain amount of shame regarding who we are and our bodies.[7] The kicker is that this shame we feel is often based on misinterpretations, but as a result, we believe we are broken. We continue using the same blueprint for everyone we meet, regardless of who it is, or how old that blueprint is. I mean, imagine using a blueprint in your 40s that you created when you were 10. It's a little outdated, don't you think?

One of the many problems with this self-shame perspective is that we think it happens only to us, so we feel alone and keep it quiet. We think if anyone knew, they'd think less of us — even though they're feeling the same thing! This is a terrible way to handle shame, because shame festers and grows in silence. The only way to weaken shame is by acknowledging it, and preferably speaking it out loud.[8] (Two resources I recommend are Brenè Brown's *Atlas of the Heart*, an insightful encyclopedia of human emotions, and Sonya Renee Taylor's book, *The Body is Not an Apology*.)

Another problem with shame is that it depletes our sense of compassion — not only for ourselves, but for others as well. It makes us impatient with people, rigid in our expectations. We begin to expect perfection — which ironically, does not exist.

What is the antidote?

Building self-awareness and practicing self-compassion. In my experience, this can be painful and emotional, like when I went through Landmark courses designed to help you identify the stories that keep you on autopilot. Or, you might remember personal experiences that were so embarrassing or shameful, you really don't care to share them with other people.

One time, in college, my friend Kim and I were on a road trip, and I made a wrong turn or missed an exit — something along those lines. It was late and dark, and I lost my temper. I got so angry that I started yelling and banging on the steering wheel. Kim, who was shocked by my behavior, simply told me, "Lis, your temper is not helping this situation. If you can't calm down, I'm going to need to get out of the car."

I was downright embarrassed! I was ashamed of losing control, of showing that side of myself. I wanted to be upset at her, but I understood then how my anger and behavior was actually impacting another person — a person I really cared about, and who mattered to me. It was a hard lesson, but an important one.

Building self-awareness doesn't have to be sad or hard, though. It can also be fun if you approach it inquisitively. I've read hundreds of excellent books (both fiction and non-fiction) over the years that spark reflection and growth. I've found that I love taking personality tests (not the ten-question quizzes in the magazines, although those can be amusing, I'll admit). Over the years, throughout my own reading and work with schools, churches, and other organizations, I've completed the assessments for Meiers-Brigg, the Four Animals, StrengthsFinder, the Enneagram, the five Love Languages, the Four Tendencies and more.

I can say that each of them offered a fairly accurate, objective description of how I operate. They're not spot on, but they usually give me great insight into what I might be doing and why. They give me a chance to wonder about myself, to see blind spots I didn't notice before, and to reflect on what aspects of myself I admire, and which I'd like to improve. They also offer a chance to see how other people think and operate, which does wonders for your relationships if you're willing to look and learn.

It's worth stating for the record: I don't believe these tests are boxes in which to place yourself, or a label to stick on your forehead, or reasons to explain your behavior, and say, for instance, "Well, I'm a worrier. That's just what my personality type does."

No, sweet girl. That would be living a very passive life. We want to live active lives that we create! These tests are not boxes; they are starting points for self-mastery, for learning to appreciate who we are and how we tick. They are tools to help us grow and become the person we want to be. It was empowering for me to learn that I like to get things done, that my impulsivity and decisiveness can be both a strength and a weakness. I liked learning – and seeing – that I am adept at managing myself, which has helped me be more patient with others who haven't yet learned that skill. I love knowing I function best with lists, structure and routines, because then I can create them wherever I am, allowing for both flexibility and success.

It's also helpful understanding which of my habits to watch out for, like my propensity to view any suggestion offered me as an obligation I must complete.[9] As an "Upholder," it's easy for me to meet expectations that I set on myself, as well as those others place on me — but sometimes it adds too much to my plate, and I get resentful, even when I'm the one agreeing to it. I've learned to take time to consider requests, rather than automatically do them.

Or, to see that my desire to get rid of what I consider "clutter" is actually hurtful to other people who think that same "clutter" is meaningful. Your brother has gotten mad at me several times for throwing away something of sentimental value to him.

Last summer, when I was with my mom, helping her sort through old pictures and memorabilia, my go-to was the garbage. I wanted to toss everything, and I became impatient when she wanted to go through it all slowly and carefully.

She became flustered, and told me quite clearly, "Lis, these may look like nothing to you, but every-thing in my house represents something special to me — a memory, a trip, a person. I will go through it all, but at my speed and I get to decide what to keep and what to toss."

As you know, MeeMa has been around for 85 years, so she's had plenty of time to accumulate these treasures. I hadn't seen them as treasures up until that point. Most of them I considered dust collectors or clutter, but when she rebuked me with that comment, I got it. She can take all the time she needs. Those are *her* things, not mine.

Personally, I appreciate how the book, "The Wisdom of the Enneagram" by Don Richard Riso explains it, and I paraphrase: We all have certain characteristics. They disintegrate when we are out of tune with ourselves, and integrate when we are in tune.[10] They allow for harmony with others and ourselves when we are conscious of these characteristics, aware of what we do and why.

Have you ever heard voices in your head, sweet girl? I'm guessing you have, and I want you to know they're normal. The critical voice that tells you that you can't, you suck, you're awful; the positive voice that tells you that you can, you're wonderful; the apprehensive voice that worries what the outcome will be; the hopeful voice that wonders if it's possible; the badass voice that is able to risk and fly instead of fall — they're all normal. Some voices are louder than others. In my experience, they are the negative ones. All of those voices, and the feelings that come with them, are part of our experience. They are part of us, yes — but they do not define us. And remember this: even when a voice is really loud in our heads, so loud that it may drown out the others, volume doesn't make it true.

The more we can recognize all the various aspects of our "selves" that live inside us simultaneously, the more balanced we will be, because we'll be better able to handle all the emotions that surface when those voices inside ourselves speak. And when we can see them for what they are — feelings, not identities — we can treat them with patience and love. We can acknowledge them, and then get back to who we want to be in our lives, in our worlds.

Remember this, Athena: No matter which voices are playing in our heads, no matter where or how the seeds of self-criticism and shame are planted, we can choose to plant other seeds, and water *those*. You will need to pick out the weeds that inevitably sprout, but the more you cultivate your mind with fertile soil, the healthier the plants that grow in your garden will be. This will only happen if you become self-aware, and start noticing those voices. It's in your best interest to start observing.

# Chapter 9

## Eager for Adventure

D ear Athena,

When I was in third grade, we moved from Rota, Spain, where Big Pop had been stationed for the last four years, to Orlando, Florida. After we moved into our home, I met some kids down the street. One of the first things I did was to ask if I could see their passport stamps. They had no idea what I was talking about. I was shocked, because I loved my passport and all the cool stamps inside, and I wanted to see theirs! I assumed everybody had one.

Thanks to growing up in my Navy family, I am very comfortable with adventure — above the ground, on the ground, and even underground. Flying "Space Available" on cargo planes to China, scuba diving in Guam, road trips around Europe, bungee jumping off a bridge in the Czech Republic, and sky diving in Oregon — those have all been activities I've enthusiastically pursued and rarely second guessed. Travel has made a huge impact on my worldview and my perspective of humanity in general. By the time I graduated college, I had visited six continents, traveled to 37 countries, and lived for extended periods of time in four of them.

College was an enjoyable time for me. I loved being on my own, asserting independence and figuring things out for myself. I liked that I knew no one there, and I met some of my truest friends for life: roommates Debbi and Dan, and amigas Stef and Molly. Since I was in Portland, Oregon, I was far enough away from my parents in Bremerton, Washington to be on my own, but close enough to go home on weekends if I wanted to see them, do some laundry, or get better (and free) food. While I have many stories from college (some fond, some I'd rather forget), I haven't included them in this book, because most of the big, impactful moments for my identity and self-worth happened in high school or before. By the time I entered and finished college, I was basically living on autopilot with that programming already running my mind.

There *is* one year of college that was very special to me, however: my junior year. That was the year I spent living abroad, the first semester in Oaxaca, Mexico; the second in Santiago de Chile.

In Mexico, I went with a group of about 30 students from Lewis & Clark College, and we all stayed with host families that were coordinated by our leader, Jack — we called him "Papa Pato" (Daddy Duck). We walked together in small packs from the neighborhoods we lived in to our classes at a language institute, and had ample time to explore markets, ruins, and restaurants. We loved the language, the ambiance, the vibe. We made friends and had romances. We visited the beaches, the bars, the dance clubs. We ate delicious food, like mole negro, tlayudas, elotes, chilaquiles, and my favorite mangos in all the world.

We didn't love it all, of course: the danger in crossing the street, the cat calls, the way that the men clustered on sidewalks would divide into two halves so that you'd have to walk between them — and then the sound of them sucking in their breath, whistling, as you walked through. Men were assertive, coming up to you directly, speaking forwardly. Others were sneaky, groping you in large crowds, so you couldn't see who it was. Still others were brazen, and insolent:  One day, a few of us (all ladies) were walking to class and this middle-aged man was standing on the brick wall lining the pedestrian walk, jeering at us as we walked by. It was only as we got closer that we saw what he was also doing: masturbating in plain sight. We were all so surprised and shocked that we just kept right on walking, doing our best to ignore him. When I told my host dad about it later that night, he gave me some advice that made me laugh: the next time that happens, you point at his penis, start laughing, and say loudly: "Eso es todo?? Qué chiquito!!!" ("Is that all? How tiny!") Thankfully, I never needed to test that particular suggestion.

The trip to Chile was different — there were about nine students from my college, many from other colleges, and we were largely on our own, attending our own classes we had signed up for in various universities. My classes were in La Universidad Católica, and La Universidad de Santiago — one private, one public; two distinct experiences. The private school ran on schedule, with very formal academic classes. The public university was quite different. For one thing, I never knew if there would be class. There were multiple times I arrived after the long bus ride to get there, only to find that classes had been canceled due to strikes happening.

School wasn't the only change between the countries. Housing was different, too. My initial host mom was a widow with a large home, which had what used to be the maid's quarters outside — that's where I stayed. As much as I appreciated having my own space, it was kind of a let down after staying with my host family in Mexico, where both the mom and dad were dentists, with three young boys, and their house had the warmth and bustle of a growing and active family. Being in the midst of all that life helped me improve my Spanish abilities quickly! When I went to Chile, I suppose I was expecting a similar experience, but I ended up isolated.

Since I didn't want to spend the next four months alone, I asked for a new host family before the deadline to request a change in host arrangements. Apparently, this made my first host very angry, perhaps because she would no longer receive the monthly stipend to pay for added expenses. I came home that Friday afternoon to see my bags thrown out of my room, the woman and her housekeeper clearing out the rest of my stuff. I asked what she was doing, and she replied that $20 were missing from inside her house, and she accused me of taking it. I had only been inside her home one time when I was being given the initial tour, so I denied the accusation. She grabbed my purse, I grabbed it back, and we engaged in a little tug of war until I was in possession of my purse. After that, she kicked me out onto the sidewalk. Where was I supposed to go?

Thankfully, I had started dating a fellow exchange student, who was with me at the time, and his host family agreed to let me stay with them for the night. As a result of their kindness, I found a new host, another widow named Irma, who lived in the same tower of condominiums that they did. Irma was delightful, a German woman who had married an Italian-Argentinian and therefore spoke German, Spanish and a little English. Under her care, I learned how to make potato gnocchi from scratch, that beets turn your poop red naturally (and there's nothing wrong, so you don't need to visit the hospital), and to laugh at the preposterous lawsuit the first mom had tried to bring against me in a Chilean court of law. After defaming my character and my college, she claimed I had hurt her shoulder in the tug of war, and then changed it to say she was suing me for emotional damage. I was more than a little unnerved by the prospect of going to court in a foreign country, but thankfully, Irma kept me rational and sane, and the judge eventually threw out the case. Phew!

Needless to say, that year was unforgettable. I vividly remember the vibrant sunsets of Santiago, the starry skies of the Southern Hemisphere, and the many adventures I took.

When I graduated from college a year later, in May 1997, I'll never forget when Papa Pato approached a group of us that had gone to Oaxaca together. He asked us all what our plans were now that we had graduated. Each person had a job lined up, or a plan of some kind… and then, he got to me. He asked, "What about you, Elisa?"

"I have no idea," I genuinely replied.

"Why don't you go back to Oaxaca? I can give you some contacts for teaching English."

And that's what I did! I got those contacts from Jack, connected with my host family and asked if I could stay with them until I found my own place. They said yes, so I moved down there and got a job teaching English —

which is how I was introduced to teaching, a career I loved for 19 years.

That wasn't the first time I had ventured out on my own, however. My very first solo trip was the summer after my 9th grade year, when my parents sent me to visit our old exchange students from Spain and Germany. First, I spent two weeks with Nieves in southern Spain, soaking up the sun by day, dancing at the discos by night, and sleeping in like a champ. I felt so rebellious telling everyone I was 16 instead of 14, and I shamelessly flirted with the cute boys vacationing from Germany, even becoming pen pals with one of them. After Spain, I traveled to Hamburg, Germany to visit Julia, where I visited her family, and in an epic side trip, attended the Pink Floyd "The Wall" concert live at the actual Berlin Wall on July 21, 1990. The "Wall," which separated communist-run East Germany and democratically-run West Germany, had fallen eight months prior, and much of it still remained. We all took pieces of the wall as mementos, and I still have a piece at home.

Travel — both with my family and alone — has taught me valuable lessons, some of which were about how to handle dangerous situations. In 1996, I traveled alone to visit my brother Todd when he lived in Prague. Afterward, I returned to Spain to see my cousin Cindy in Madrid, and then embarked on a solo tour of Sevilla, Granada, and other cities in the southern half of Spain. I took the bus to get around, and taxis to get to hostels or hotels when they weren't close enough to walk.

One day, I arrived to a city and caught a taxi to the hotel. Always one to practice my Spanish, I started chatting with the driver, and when we arrived at the hotel, he insisted on carrying my backpack in for me — first red flag. Once I checked in, he insisted on going up the elevator with me and walking me to my room — second, and brighter, red flag. He even tried to come into my room — third, fiery red flag — but I said no, I needed to rest. Once that door was shut, my gut instinct was firing on all cylinders, screaming, "Get out of here!"

I waited a few moments, collected myself, grabbed my bag, and hailed another taxi to take me right back to the bus station from which I had just come, and caught a bus out of town. I'm glad I listened to my gut that day. I have no idea if he was waiting for me anywhere, or would come back, but I wasn't going to stay and find out. I wish I had known the "you can just say no" lesson your dad taught me years later, because I would have used it that first moment when the taxi driver wanted to carry my bag for me. I may have avoided some more harmful incident by leaving that hotel. Whether I did or didn't actually doesn't matter. What does matter is that I listened to my instincts. Trust your gut, sweet girl. When you sense danger, *leave*. (Side note: another reason to lift weights and strengthen your body is so that you can carry your own dang bags. No help needed!)

When I lived in Oaxaca the second time, on my own as a teacher, I had another scary situation. One afternoon, as I was walking home after morning classes for lunch, a group of 4-5 young men started following me. I kept my distance, and paid attention to what they were doing. As I picked up the pace, they picked up the pace. When I crossed the road, they crossed the road. They started making suggestive and lewd comments, and truly, I became frightened. I wondered what I would do at the Y in the road coming up — to the left was my apartment, to the right was unknown territory. I didn't want to go right, because I didn't know where it would lead, or what I would find there. If they took the left to follow me, I couldn't go home. I'd have to keep walking and go somewhere else. Thankfully, they veered right when I went left, but let me tell you, honey love, your mama was shaken. I learned to always pay attention to my surroundings, and go into public places when you're being followed.

Other incidents have happened on airplanes I never would have imagined. For instance, once I traveled to Kentucky for a family reunion. Somehow I contracted the stomach flu moments before the trip, and I spent most of the flight in the airplane lavatory, either vomiting or mildly catatonic. Everyone who saw me did one of those

"Whoa" back up moves to give me as wide a girth as possible.

Two other experiences threw me for such a loop that I didn't know how to handle them, mainly because I didn't know how to stick up for myself back then. Once, as an older teenager, I was on a red-eye flight with hardly any passengers — there were many more vacant seats than occupied. While this was great for trying to sleep, I've never been a great sleeper on planes, so I was sitting up much of the time, reading. This was back in the day when they handed out blankets to each passenger, and one man a few rows in front of me decided to expose his penis to me under his blanket. I quickly moved to some seats a few rows in front of him. Would you believe *he* moved again, a few seats in front of me, so he could fondle himself again, I assume with the hopes of me watching. It was disturbing to say the least. If I hadn't been so young at the time, I would have pushed that "call attendant" button and told them what was going on immediately. I hope nothing like that ever happens to you, sweet girl, but if it does, don't keep quiet about it! Stand up and say something loud, along the advice my Mexican host dad gave me. Something like, "Why are you showing your penis on an airplane?"

Another time, in my twenties, I was on a flight to San Diego, sitting in the middle seat, and the guy in the window seat started a conversation. At first it was interesting — he was a welder, flying from Louisiana to see a friend. He had brought some crawfish to share with that friend, and he offered to get me some from his bag in the overhead bin. I politely declined. That part could be considered normal conversation, I suppose. But then, he explained he was also a massage therapist, that he'd be happy to give me a rub while I was in San Diego. My friend, too, if she'd like. (How generous!) He complimented me on my beauty, even though I was wearing no makeup and had a giant volcano of a zit on my forehead that day (I remember, because I had tried to pop it and ended up making it even larger and redder). He asked me what my favorite sex positions were (excuse me??), and also offered his shoulder to lean on in case I wanted to take a nap on the flight. I wish there were some open seats on *that* flight, because I would've moved in a heartbeat. Alas, that wasn't an option. And, since I was so afraid of offending someone, I just sat there and took it. If I could go back in time, I'd instate a simple boundary using the examples Melissa Urban gave me,[11] "This conversation feels inappropriate to me, and I'm going to stop talking to you now."

It's crazy to think that most of my solo travel was done in the era before cell phones and internet — we barely had email. We definitely didn't have any instant communication, or GPS, or apps that could help us find a hotel, restaurant, or taxi. Sometimes I wonder how I did it, how my parents survived without worrying themselves sick about me, as I imagine I would with you or Michael if you went on such trips by yourselves.

But then, I remember, they had even less than we did! (My dad spent one of his college summers backpacking around Europe, and ended up as a chocolate taste-tester for the Lindt factory. How fun is that?) It seems terrifying now, but we didn't know any other alternative. And maybe that was a good thing. Sometimes it feels like we are so reliant on outside sources (like social media sites, internet, and phones) to do our thinking for us, that we don't know to think for ourselves, how to get in touch with ourselves, or even to be with ourselves.

Why do I love travel so much? Maybe because it helps me get present to what's around me. It helps me SEE. There's fresh perspective on people and places. New things to learn, new foods to taste, new languages to hear. I suppose I also liked that *I* could start fresh, too, without the baggage from my past. Which is a lie, to some extent, because you carry that baggage with you, no matter where you go. (I've heard the joke that the goal is simply to deal with your baggage so that it goes from a few suitcases to one carry-on size.)

But it's not just travel that I love — it's really adventure. Travel is simply a way to experience adventure, but so is scuba diving, snorkeling, sky diving, bungee jumping, and more. Now, as a mom of two kids in school, adventures look a little different. Of course we had our two years of nomadic life, but things closer to home can be adventures, also — new jobs, new restaurants, new recipes, new activities, new animals spotted, new plants potted, even a new route to school.

So, sweet girl, consider adventure as one of your greatest teachers. Spontaneity can be a wonderful gift, as can planning ahead. I encourage you to have both in your life. You never know what doors might open. If one opens, push it a bit and see what opens up for you. If you like what you see, take a few steps forward. If you don't, move along and another will open. Whatever adventure you take, or wherever you explore, know there will be wonders ahead, as well as some risk, or even danger. That's okay, as long as you can navigate it. This is another reason I want you to know yourself and be comfortable with your feelings, because it's critical for your well-being that you are able to trust yourself. Plan ahead when you can, go with your gut when you can't. You are capable, and you can do it.

# PART THREE:

## Demolition

*"Your task is not to seek for love, but merely to seek and find all the barriers within yourself that you have built against it."*[12]

-Helen Schucman

*"I'm working on my own life story. I don't mean I'm putting it together; no, I'm taking it apart."*[13]

-Margaret Atwood

# Chapter 10

## The Crumbling Chameleon

D ear Athena,

I wish I could say that after my dad's death, I had a "Phoenix Rising" moment, where I finally got it and figured it all out. In reality, it was more like leveling a skyscraper down to its foundation. Before you can build again, first you have to demolish. Then you have to clear away the rubble, which, so you know, takes much longer than destroying. It took quite some time to clear my foundation enough to even see it.

At the root of my lack of identity and self-love were my chameleon tendencies of fitting in wherever I went, combined with my achiever tendencies. You tell me what it means to be "good" at something, and I'll do it.

First, there was my Christianity, which I had converted to, or had been "born again" when I was teaching at a middle school in Tualatin, Oregon. My friend Lisa had invited me multiple times to her church, and at a Christmas dessert event, I declared Jesus as my savior. It was genuine, but I felt I had to prove it — what did being a good Christian mean?

- Bible Study. I enrolled.

- Memorizing scripture. I began a routine of daily, weekly, and monthly repetition that endured for years, memorizing hundreds of verses.

- Mission trips. I completed several.

- Daily Bible reading. I read it through, front to back, multiple times.

- Tithing. Consider it done.

- No more sex until marriage. Okay, but seriously? That part was almost a relief.

I even took a job with the high school ministry at the church, where I worked happily for several years. I enrolled in seminary, found it intriguing, and thoroughly enjoyed those studies.

However, when my dad died, I wondered where he was. He had not declared Jesus as his savior. In fact, after my conversion, he surprised me during one of his visits in Beaverton when he told me that, while he admired my faith, he believed that when we die, our bodies rot in the ground, and nothing else happens. This shocked me, because we grew up going to church, his mom was a devout Christian, his grandfather was a Nazarene pastor, and he encouraged me to take the job at the church instead of teaching, despite the pay cut. Since finances were a matter of importance to him, I always took this as support of my faith, which it was, but also a sign of his own faith, which it clearly wasn't.

I remembered this conversation after he had died and worried — Where was he? Was he in hell? It couldn't be. My dad was the only reason I could believe in a Heavenly Father, one who is loving unconditionally, but also just. How could I believe in a God who would condemn my father to hell?

The answer is, I couldn't. That caused me a lot of angst. I still worked at the church, and I had nightmares where my dad would visit me and speak in cryptic ways that left me worrying that he was suffering, in pain, and putting on a good face to ease my anxiety. It didn't.

During this time I went in for my annual checkup, which typically went well because I was in good shape and healthy. This time, however, my liver numbers came back looking like an alcoholic's liver, and my cholesterol was high.

My physician asked, "Have you been drinking a lot?"

I said no — because it was true. I was dating a man at the time who did not drink, and I was doing CrossFit, so I didn't drink at all. Thinking it was perhaps my diet,

I cut out eggs and started eating a lot of oatmeal, the traditional remedy for high cholesterol (now we know your dietary cholesterol doesn't impact your body's cholesterol, by the way, so keep eating those eggs). We scheduled an appointment in six months to check my numbers again.

Towards the end of those six months, I went on a writing retreat through a different church, where we practiced dialogue with important figures in our lives. For me, those dialogues were with the church, God, and my dad.

At the beginning of the retreat, the vision I had of myself was a blind bat, wildly flying and trying to find her way to wherever it was she was supposed to be. Somehow, I had lost my sense of echolocation, and was disoriented. This made sense to me, since the loss of my father had profoundly impacted my sense of self.

By the end of the retreat, I had a vision of two bearded men, arms wrapped around the others' shoulders, both smiling widely, joyously looking down on their daughter, with whom they were well pleased. I instantly understood that those bearded men were my dad and God.

My heart and mind were brought immense peace by that vision. The nightmares stopped. Lo and behold, at my next checkup, both my liver numbers and cholesterol had returned to normal. Did you know that our body can actually store grief and trauma? Our bodies truly *are* connected to our minds, sweet girl, and our souls, too.

Around that time, I stopped working for the church. I left my seminary studies, too. This isn't to say I left my faith, because I didn't; it simply became mine, something more intimate and personal. I went back to teaching, and that cleared away a little of the rubble.

The second issue was the man I was dating at the time. He was a good person, thoughtful, and handy. We had met through a friend, and we began dating before my dad died. He was a wonderful knight in shining armor, and he had two big moments to pull through for me: when I broke my wrist and needed surgery, and when my dad died. The rest of the time in our relationship, I didn't need or want a rescuer.

I was an independent, capable woman, but I also wanted a husband, a partner — and I still had those chameleon tendencies. When I dated men, I tried to figure out what they wanted from me and then do whatever that was. With my ex, he wasn't sure what he wanted from me, and I wasn't sure what I was or who I was, so he came and went — and I took him back, repeatedly. Perhaps it wasn't fair of me to look to someone else to tell me what I should be; of course it wasn't — no one can do that for us, but it was all I knew to do. And perhaps he didn't know what he wanted, either. One of my friends described our relationship as if he eclipsed me, leaving only my edges visible behind him; another described it as him saying he really loved cherry pie, but then when he got it, he scooped out all the filling. Our relationship was on again, off again, and never really happy. We were both Christians trying to push the limits on what was sexually acceptable, we both really wanted it to work, and we wanted to be with someone, but it wasn't working because we were not well-matched.

The Thanksgiving after my dad died, he proposed. We were at a riverbank in one of the most picturesque places in Oregon, and as he knelt, I had a sinking feeling deep in my heart. I knew what he was going to say, and that it wasn't a good idea, but I ignored it. I willed that voice to be quiet, and when he asked, "Will you marry me?" I said, "Yes."

Thankfully, our pattern of on again /off again contin-ued, and he broke up with me again, stating the obvious: we were miserable. It's true, we were. I knew this was my chance to listen to that instinct I felt when he had proposed. This time, when he came back, I recognized that weight in my heart, and I was strong enough to resist him, and honor my own soul. It was one of the most difficult things I have done. When he insisted on our reconciliation, I told him I would consider our rela-tionship for 40 days, without contact, and then we would reconnect. During those 40 days of reflection, each time I thought about reconciling with him, I physically felt a weight compress my chest. Every time I considered being single, I felt free and light. At the end of the 40 days, I honored my *self*. I pushed aside the fear that I would be alone forever, and recognized it would be better to be on my own than feel suffocated or trapped in a relationship. I chose levity and freedom, and that decision cleared away more of the rubble.

Religion and relationships were big mounds of rubble I needed to remove from my foundation, so that I could build a new structure, based on my beliefs — which I didn't yet know exactly what they were, but somehow, I trusted I would find them. It would take years longer, with other stops and starts, to be able to truly see that home being built, but I had a vision: a modest, cozy home, with room for growth — just the way I like it.

What I want you to understand from these stories, sweet girl, is that I don't regret them. They were all steps along my path, teaching and guiding me. My life has turned out the way it has, and it can only be the way it is right now, given the circumstances, choices, and understanding that has led me to this point. You, too, will have experiences that challenge you, and make you wonder if you're losing yourself. And I want you to know, Athena, that as long as you stay connected to that soul inside you, as long as you honor your self, and wonder what she wants, how she feels safe, and what will help her stay true — you will keep yourself.   There are no wrong choices, only choices, and you will move along the path that each choice illuminates for you. Trust yourself, sweet girl, and the next move will become clear.

# Chapter 11

## My Food Matters?

D ear Athena,
Growing up I understood that eating vegetables was good for you. I ate them, but only the ones my dad liked: mushy ones. GROSS. Needless to say, I didn't eat many. Once I was in high school, my mom and I often made our own broccoli (which he didn't like, but we did), just so we could have some variety along with the spinach salads we ate. Lima beans and corn were also considered veggies, and I'm not sure if I ate any veggies in college, to be honest!

Before Dad's death, I used to go Bally's Gym, one of those big box gyms that are full of machines and weights, open from 5am to 11pm. I had my routine of three days I would rotate: back & biceps, leg day, chest & triceps. My dad was the one who had first taken me to the Navy gym to teach me how to use the machines, what to do at the gym, and give me some ideas of how to do it on my own, which I did throughout college and beyond.

But once he died, it was as if all my energy was gone. I walked into the gym, as usual, but I had no idea what to do. It seemed pointless, like a pencil with no lead.

Back in those days, we had paper coupon books — entire books organized by sections like Dining Out, Health, Groceries, Activities, etc, where you could get coupons for things like "60 minutes kayak rental free," or "buy one entree, get one 50% off" — things like that. Well, I found one for a discounted introductory week at a local CrossFit gym.

What's funny about that is my boyfriend at that time was, in fact, a CrossFit coach, and he had invited me to his gym multiple times, but I never wanted to go. I considered it to be "his" thing. I thought it was too expensive, and, honestly, I was intimidated. The one time I did go, I ended up breaking my right wrist and having surgery. (That's another story, but suffice it to say that you should always pay attention to the various heights of pull-up bars and make sure no wooden boxes are nearby if you decide to jump and reach a bar, because you might miss it, fall and crack your wrist on said box, and then need surgery and have to wear a cast cover for the entire trip to Hawaii you had just bought tickets for that very same morning.)

With that coupon, I decided to give CrossFit a shot. What I found surprised me.

First, I found Rochelle, a coach so warm and welcoming that I ended up sharing with her about my dad's death a month prior. She hugged me, coached me, and understood when my workouts would often end in tears. Those workouts were not only empowering, they were cathartic as well.

Second, the community was unlike any I had ever known. People from all careers and backgrounds coming together to get stronger in body and mind. The focus on growth, friendly encouragement, and new friends was exactly what I needed.

Third, they cared about my body, and its ability to move. CrossFit prioritizes functional movement patterns, promoting strength, flexibility, and endurance. Through varied workouts, it aims to enhance overall fitness, which reduces injury risk and improves long-term mobility for everyday activities and athletic performance. I wanted all of that, and it felt good, too, even if it was hard. I appreciate how the movements they teach require you to use your body and brain simultaneously, which is the way we seem to have been designed to use them. As authors John Matey and Richard Manning put it, humans are the Swiss Army Knives of animals, and the more we can move our whole bodies and minds, the better for our health.[14]

And fourth, they cared about my nutrition. Food wasn't a reward, or a punishment; it was fuel. They were the first people to open my eyes to how the Standard American

Diet of highly processed food provided very little in terms of actual nourishment. They offered a cookbook following the Paleo Diet that Rochelle's husband Scott had written, and a challenge to help us practice those recipes as a way of life.

I accepted the challenge, and I couldn't believe my transformation. My body became a lean, efficient machine, capable of things I had not accomplished before, and some I had never even heard of: Pull ups! Snatches! Double unders! Muscle ups!

Never mind that 14 years later I can't do muscle ups or double unders anymore (although I'm getting better at them). I was doing them then, and it was empowering. I marveled at how good my body felt, how strong it became, how muscular and capable it was. I felt incredible!

My physical prowess made me feel stronger emotionally, too. Of course I missed my dad awfully, but I slowly became more confident in my ability to stand alone; that I could be myself, once I figured out who that was.

CrossFit showed me I could. It proved that the human mind and body were stronger than the things that happened to it, and that I was the only one who could push and grow myself beyond my current limitations — no one else could do that for me.

It also taught me that my body was far more than something to look good — it was my vessel, the vehicle I had to experience the world, and I could choose to strengthen it (or not), and fuel it well (or not). I began to understand that the quality of my life depended on the health of my body *and* mind, and how interlaced those two things really are. I wanted my physical health to match my cognitive health, as Dr. Lisa Mosconi puts it.[15]

CrossFit helped me start living with that long-term goal in mind — not only because of the exercises, but because of the food. It was my first step into the world of truly understanding nutrition. I learned my food *did* matter — to my body *and* my brain. It heavily impacted the way I felt, how I acted, and my ability to perform. I was learning to keep them both sharp and honed. I began to wonder, why not maximize this nutrition thing? And I did, over the next several years, with nutrition certificates, courses, and other studies.

I learned how the same nutrition that is good for my metabolic health, my heart health, and overall body's health is also good for my brain health. No matter what our bodies look like, no matter if we are battling a sickness, or have an amputated limb, or dealing with degenerative illnesses like Parkinson's or Lou Gehrig's disease... no matter what hand our bodies are dealt, your food choices actively impact your overall health. Foods that keep your metabolism (and heart and brain) in good working order are wild protein sources, a variety of vegetables, healthy fats from seafood, nuts, seeds, avocados and olives, and some unrefined carbohydrates, like tubers, fruits, and whole grains. Foods that slow it down and can cause multiple issues over time are the refined and processed foods we find so easily in stores, and look nothing like the plant from which they come. What you eat becomes the raw materials your cells use to create new cells,[16] so why wouldn't you want to give your body the highest quality material you can?

I'm not saying you have to do CrossFit, sweet girl. I *am* saying you need to find some combination of exercise and movement that stimulates you, so that both your brain and body are alert and working. I am also saying that you will have a chance to use food either to inhibit or invigorate your body. It's oh-so-tempting to eat more of the comfort foods than it is the nutritious ones. It's easy, too. In fact, it's what will happen unless you intentionally choose to eat the nutrient-dense foods more frequently than the rest, until that becomes second nature to you. Remember, eating nutrient-dense, fresh whole foods doesn't make you a good person. What it *does* do, my love, is give your body and brain higher chances to *thrive*. Good health won't be a possibility for you, it will be a probability — and *that* will boost your quality of life, and the way you experience it, immensely.

# Chapter 12

## Sourdough Pancakes

Dear Athena,

As I've mentioned before, breakfasts growing up — at least during the weekdays — were always cereal. On Saturday or Sunday, though, my dad, your Big Pop, would make a special breakfast. In the spring or summer, it could be sourdough crepes, when fresh berries were plentiful. Occasionally we'd get banana bread. Most weekends, though, it was banana sourdough pancakes. My dad would make each batch fresh so they were piping hot; he even warmed our plates in the oven, and the syrup as well, so the pancakes would stay warm on our plates as long as possible. They were delicious, made with love, and I loved them. I was delighted that he continued this weekend breakfast tradition whenever I was home visiting from college or beyond.

One weekend as a young adult, I had come to visit because a former high school friend was getting married in Seattle. I went to the wedding, drank way too much alcohol, slept overnight there, and returned to my parents' house the next morning via the ferry. After all the celebrating, I was suffering from a major hangover.

I walked into the kitchen around 10:00 a.m. My dad heard the door open, spun around on his feet, and flashing his big grin, said, "There she is!"

He had his apron on, a spatula in his right hand, and I could see the griddle on the counter behind him. "Perfect timing! Pancakes are ready."

I looked at his eager face and knew he had made these pancakes just for me. I wanted to enjoy them, but I knew at that moment I physically couldn't stomach them, and I knew I would let him down when I told him why.

You see, sweet girl, Big Pop didn't drink alcohol. Not a drop. Apparently he had, once or twice in college, but he hated the sensation of losing control of himself, so he never did again. I believe his dad also drank, and there were alcoholic tendencies that ran through the family, so he avoided it. It was evident to me he thought alcohol was a waste of time and money — utterly useless.

To make matters worse, I had a negative track record with my dad and alcohol. I actually didn't really enjoy drinking, but I did enjoy the feeling of being drunk, of not caring, of having no inhibitions —and doing what everyone else was doing. At my high school the cool kids drank; therefore, so did I. I got in a fair amount of trouble, too.

When I was a senior, the night of the Sweetheart Swirl dance, there was an after-party at my date's house (we were just friends). I drank two bottles of Boone's wine cooler (it was very popular back in 1993), then decided I would spend the night at my friend Tawnya's house. To do that, though, I'd need to go to my house and get clothes for the next day, because I was expected to be at church in the morning. So, Tawnya and I drove to my house, and after I quietly gathered a few things, I got in my car to go to her house, so that I could drive myself to church the next day. Tawnya followed me, and it's a good thing she did. It must have been around 1:30 in the morning, and it was cold and drizzly — as is the usual weather in the Pacific Northwest in February. The roads were dark, slick, and I was speeding — not a good combination.

I was familiar with the residential roads near my home, so I curved around the bend and then accelerated to go up the slight hill at the next bend, running the stop sign so I could keep momentum. In doing so, I lost control of the car, and it went up one of the thick wire cables holding up the telephone pole. My car flipped and landed upside down, on the opposite side of the street. The roof was crushed, preventing the doors from opening. The side windows had shattered, the windshield had cracked, and the back windshield was gone completely. (Later, I'd learn the horn still worked.) If you looked at the wreckage, you would be shocked to hear that I was unhurt. (That's the benefit of seat belts, sweet girl, so *please, always* wear yours.) Except for the scratches on my hands and knees that I received while crawling over the broken shards of the back window, which was the only way I could escape the upturned car, I was physically unharmed.

At the same time that I was crawling out of my crumpled car, Tawnya was coming around the bend. She saw me, and after registering what had happened and making sure I was okay, she went to go get my parents.

My dad was a captain in the Navy. I was an honors student. He didn't drink. And there I was, his only daughter, driving drunk. My dad didn't get angry — more often, he would be "disappointed," which was far worse for me. I was sobbing hysterically by the time my parents arrived, not only because I knew I would get in massive trouble with the cops, but because I feared I would lose the respect and love of my dad. I knew he'd be utterly disappointed.

Mom, or MeeMa, was there too. As you know, she is nearly deaf, so when she heard I had drunk two bottles of Boone's, she heard two bottles of "booze," so she began getting hysterical herself, saying we needed to get me to the hospital to pump my stomach. I'm pretty sure Tawnya was trying to calm her down while I was with my dad and the cops who had arrived. I had damaged someone else's property, totaled the car, and thankfully, mercifully, had not hurt anyone, including myself.

I was asked to walk a line, touch my nose, recite my ABCs, all of which I did compliantly. It was apparent to everyone how remorseful I was. I can only guess that the police officer knew I'd get in a heap of trouble for this at home, and since I hadn't hurt anyone, he gave me a court date with the charge of negligent driving – which was a much lighter citation than either reckless driving or driving under the influence, both of which I deserved. It was a generous kindness and act of mercy on his part.

I was grounded, unable to drive, and had a curfew for weeks. Once I was allowed to drive again, I could only do so after signing a contract my dad had created, spelling out consequences for future infractions.

That night brought on a whole new wave of shame, another layer of shame added to the one I had already collected when I contracted HPV the year before. I felt shame not only driving drunk, which I knew was dangerous and foolish (I was young and often thoughtless, thinking things like this wouldn't happen to me), but also for ruining the image my Dad held of his daughter, yet again. I knew I had *again* not done what he had expected of me. My value was diminished even *further* in his eyes. I was no longer a good daughter.

I believed my dad felt the same way, because *I* felt it so strongly. Our feelings sometimes get the best of us, sweet girl. The feelings and emotions we feel are so strong, we believe they *must* be accurate. We don't even consider they could be wrong. I was 17 at that time, and from that point on I lived believing I was "less than" in my parents' eyes — I was a disappointment.

Did it stop me from drinking? Absolutely not. Did it keep me distant from my parents? Yes. Did I do better at living my chameleon lifestyle, being one way in the presence of my parents, another at school, and another with friends? You'd better believe it.

I've since learned the science of how alcohol affects your brain. (My thanks to Malcolm Gladwell and his educational description of alcohol's effects in his book, "Talking to Strangers.")[17] First, it impacts your frontal lobe, the part of your brain that is involved in attention, motivation, planning and learning — alcohol makes you less able to think through things that require more consideration. Then it slows down your amygdala, which is the part of your brain that tells you whether or not you are in danger. Next, it hits the reward center of your brain, so that you feel pleasure. If you have enough of it, alcohol then impacts your hippocampus, which is involved in your memory, which leads to blackouts, where you actually can still be functioning, but not remember a single thing you do during that time.

Alcohol impacts the brains of both males and females, essentially putting us in situations where we are not as able to perceive threats, where we think less about future consequences, all while feeling good and potentially impacting our memory of the experience. Needless to say, this can drastically increase the chances of things happening that wouldn't happen if people were sober. Sadly, I can say that I have had multiple instances where I experienced both blackouts and events I never would have agreed to had I been sober.

Women *do* need to be more cognizant about our alcohol consumption, by the way. It is technically a poison for all genders, albeit a socially acceptable one. However, women actually metabolize alcohol more slowly than men, because we have less water in our bodies, which means it enters our bloodstream faster. As a result, we can have higher blood alcohol content with fewer drinks.

Back to the story. That Sunday morning, 15 years after the Sweetheart Swirl incident, when I walked in after the wedding and saw my dad's beaming face, offering me pancakes he had made with love, it broke my heart to tell him the truth:

"Thank you, Dad. I would really love to have some, but I drank way too much last night, and I am very hungover right now. All I can do is sleep. I'm so sorry."

Can you guess what he did?

My dad surprised the heck out of me when he looked at me and said, "You go rest, Lis. The pancakes will be here when you get up." I could hear in his voice he meant it. He was gentle and kind, not angry or disappointed as I imagined he would be.

I didn't realize in the moment why I was so grateful for that response, but I do now: it's because that was the first time I had done something I *knew* my dad disapproved of, but I also knew he still loved me. I was brave enough to be honest, and, in return, he showed me love.

Realizing that his love could be unconditional, that I could be loved even if I *hadn't* produced the desired result, or been the way I thought I was *supposed* to be — that cracked open the door to being able to love myself, seeing myself in a gentler, more compassionate light. That interaction became the first baby step I took towards self-love.

Sweet girl, I want you to know right now that there is *nothing* you could do, or not do, that would make me love you less. You are worthy of love, simply for being *you*. And your mama finally believes that for herself, too.

# Chapter 13

---

# You Can Just Say No

D ear Athena,
     The first real conversation I had with your dad
will stay with me always. He had recently joined the
CrossFit gym, and we had started noticing when the
other person was going to class. Wouldn't you know, we
both soon began going to either the 4:00pm or 5:00pm
class, because that's when the other one would be there.

One afternoon, your dad arrived and I was outside, doing a different workout, alone. He walked up and asked,
"What are you doing out here?"

"I'm doing the competition WOD," I replied. (The competition WOD was the workout for people who were
competing on the gym team for the annual CrossFit
Games.)

He astutely observed, "Well, you don't look very happy
about it."

I admitted, "I'd rather be inside doing the workout with
everyone else."

And then he asked me a truly thought-provoking question: "Then why did you say yes?"

That question flustered me; I didn't know how to respond. I had said yes because they wanted me to be on the team. Did *I* really want to be on the team? I didn't really consider that. This was another example of me doing what I thought I needed to do so that I would be liked, approved of, or accepted. I thought competing was what a "good Crossfitter" would do.

Ben looked at me, a little amused, and said casually, "You know you can say no, right?"

I must have stared at him blankly, because the next words out of his mouth were, "Here, let's role play."

Perplexed, I listened to him explain how he was going to act as one of the gym coaches, and I would be me, and then he launched into an outstanding impersonation:

"Elisa — we see your dedication at the gym. You've been coming here for a year now and making incredible progress. You're clearly in great shape, you've got great energy, and we really think you'd be an asset to our team. We need another female and we think you'd be the perfect fit. What do you say? Will you join our competition team?"

Caught off guard by his intensity, I started stammering things like, "Wow, uh... it's such an honor to be asked... thank you for the compliment... I – I'd love to, but I really think I'd rather stick with the regular gym classes... I'm not sure I'd be able to keep up..." and a few other excuses.

Ben quietly interrupted, saying, "You can just say, 'No, thanks.' You don't have to explain."

That's all I recall about that conversation. Up until that point, I had simply noticed your dad's big, bright smile, but after that conversation, I wondered, "Who the heck *is* this guy?"

He had just given me a very important lesson on how not to be a people pleaser, and on how to honor myself. That was my second critical lesson on learning to love myself.

What I've learned since then is that I still need practice saying "No, thanks," but I'm getting better at it. Many books have helped me along the way, including "The Year of Yes" by Shonda Rhimes, which taught me that if I was going to say yes to something, then make sure it was a "hell yeah!" not an "okay, I guess so."[18]

From Jim Kwik's book "Limitless" I learned how to identify my values and align my behaviors to them.[19] I've gotten really clear on what matters to me, and thanks to James Clear[20] and Benjamin Hardy,[21] I've learned how to optimize my choices and environment to protect my focus and those things that matter most.

I also learned that integrity doesn't necessarily mean honesty or morality, or the way you act when no one is looking. That's part of it, sure, and another way to look at integrity refers more to functionality, and I'm grateful to the courses I took with Landmark Worldwide for their perspective on integrity. Integrity is really about what *works*.

For instance, if a four-legged stool had one leg removed, how much integrity does that stool still have? How reliable is it to sit on? How well can that stool do its job?[22] The same applies to me. What are my jobs? What do I want to be able to do? Where do I want to spend my time? How will my "yes" or "no" answer affect my ability to stay true to my integrity, my ability to do what I believe I was put here to do? Will my life function well if I do? If my answer hinders my ability to function well, then it's out of integrity for me.

I want my answer (and your answer) to the things asked of me to support my integrity — the workings of my life — regardless of whether they are done in public or in private. If I do things that "work" for my values, then I'm being honest and authentic, which, of course, is also integrity.

It was difficult to say no. It's a skill I still practice, and one I've only recently felt comfortable doing. I still say yes to many things, but it feels good to say "no" when needed.

I want *you* to be able to say "No, thank you" as often as you need to, sweet girl. Take some time to consider your values, what matters to you, what makes you feel alive. Say *yes* to the things that light you up, that grow you as a person, and fill you up. Say *no* to the things that will deplete you, make you doubt yourself, or dim your brightness. And remember what your daddy told me: no explanation is needed. You can just say, "No."

# Chapter 14

## What Do YOU Want?

D ear Athena,
    Let's continue talking about your dad for a moment, because he's been one of my greatest teachers and supporters.

When we were first dating, I was trying to figure him out. I still had those chameleon tendencies I mentioned earlier. My regular mode of operation was to figure out what a guy wanted from me, and then do that. Was it sex? Cooking? Scripture memorization? Watching TV? What did a good girlfriend look like to that guy? My goal was to learn what that was and be that person.

I don't recommend this approach, sweet girl. While I thought it would bring happiness, it most certainly did not. Instead, it sets you up for a whole lot of pain, heartache, and far too many boundary issues. Plus, you never get to appreciate *your*self, and what *you* bring to the relationship. (Knowing you, that's a whole lot to offer.)

With your dad, however, I could *not* get a good read on what he was looking for in a woman. In fact, one day during a picnic we had taken on the grassy lawns of Portland's southwest waterfront, I got so frustrated that I blurted out, "What do you want from me?! Who do you want me to be?!?"

Ben looked at me, eyes wide in surprise, and said simply, "I want you to be you."

The problem was, I didn't know who that was. I mean, I knew I was a teacher, but beyond that, who was I?

- What would you do with a million dollars?

- If you won the lottery, what would you do with the money?

- If fear or money weren't an issue, what would you do with your life?

These are the kinds of questions your dad would ask me, and at first I had no answer. I thought they were ridiculous and superfluous. These situations were never going to happen, so why even ask?

The reason we ask these kinds of questions, and ponder the various answers, is because they show us our hearts' desires. When we follow our hearts, we connect with our soul. When we connect with our soul, we get in touch with ourselves, and then we can begin to live freely.

Let me explain. When I say "soul," I am referring to your uniqueness, the essence of who you are. It's your personality, your energy, your aura, your passions, your body, your desires, your value... all of that and more. It's really your SELF.

Did you know that when we die, we lose about three pounds? I learned this from neuroscientist Dr. Caroline Leaf. When we die, three pounds of *us* disappears.[23] Nothing has changed physically. We haven't lost blood, or muscle, or an organ. What we *have* lost is the life force that makes us who we are. Our energy. Our soul.

Isn't that remarkable? Did you also know that your brain has 200 specializations unique to YOU, and that no one else will have that combination of 200 special-izations?[24] YOU are truly a gift. YOU have value just by being YOU, not by anything you do. Or anything you earn, have, say, look like, or become.

That was a hard message for me to hear, much less believe. I had lived my whole life operating under the philosophy that I am only as good as what I produce — what I have to show for it. My grades, my body, my results, my evaluations at work, my performance at the gym. "What do you mean, I have value even if I never DO anything? Yeah, right. That's a load of baloney. Pshh!"

And then I became a mother, first to Michael, and then to you.

When the topic came up again, again I dismissed it. And then I was asked, "Elisa, would you still love your kids, even if they never went to college, got a job, or 'did' anything?"

I replied, "Yes, of course!" Of *course* I would. And it dawned on me. You and Michael don't have to *do* anything, *be* anything, *say* anything, *look* a certain way, or become *anything* for me to love you wholeheartedly. I love you for who you are, *no matter what.*

That got me wondering, *could* that also be true of me? *Could* I be loved for who I am, no matter what? And somewhere, deep inside myself, what I believe to be my soul, whispered, "YES!" My soul *wanted* me to start loving it again, and I believe yours does, too.

And even though it seemed absolutely ridiculous to me, that little tug from my soul was enough to ask myself the question: "How would I treat myself if I DID love myself? If I honored my soul?"

The answer was: *very* differently than the way I had been treating myself, that's for sure. I had always been trying to control everything, dropping the hammer on myself whenever I did anything that wasn't perfect. Always expecting more from myself. Making nutrition choices not because they were *good* for me, but because of the way they would make me *look*. Depriving myself.

Feeling like I was missing out on something good, and berating myself for it. And then when I wasn't depriving myself, feeling like I was doing something wrong. So self-critical. So judgmental. So harsh. So unloving.

I had to ask myself: Would I *ever* treat my children that way? My best friend? My husband? Those answers were an easy and resounding, "NO." I would never! If I did, I'm guessing we wouldn't have a close relationship very long, or at all. And yet, there I was, treating myself dismally every single day.

That, sweet girl, is not respecting your soul. That is repressing your soul. That is dominating your soul. That is imprisoning your soul.

To let our souls FLY, we have to undo what binds them. The list of chains linked to our soul is a long one: our experiences, media influence, trauma, short-term mentality, diet culture, shame, and dichotomous thinking, to name only a handful.

Dichotomous thinking is the tendency to think in terms of opposite categories—that is, in terms of the best and worst—without accepting that there are many possibilities that lie in between these two extremes. Here are some examples:

- good / bad

- right / wrong

- off / on

- succeed / fail

- flawless / defective

- saint / sinner

- now / never

- win / lose

- either / or

I was an expert at dichotomous thinking. The problem is, when we have dichotomous thoughts, we tend to view mildly negative events as extremely negative, instead of looking at them as things that simply happen, and maybe, just maybe, they don't mean *anything*!

Dichotomous thinking contributes to dissatisfaction in many areas of life, because it can cause overreactions or emotional responses that can impact relationships, work environments, achieving goals, and our quality of life in general. They cause us to give up before we're finished, often before we've even given ourselves a chance.

Those chains like shame, dichotomous thoughts, and media messages trick us into believing we don't belong, that we're broken, that we'll never measure up. They imprison your soul. But guess what? Your soul *does* belong. Your soul is YOU.

As I've told you and your brother many, many times at bedtime: You are compassionate. You are thoughtful. You are generous. You are important. Your voice matters.

Read carefully here, sweet girl: There is *nothing* in those 200 unique specializations about you that needs to be hidden from this world, because together they make you, *you.* That means you are perfect, whole, and complete just the way you are, *and* the way you are not. Is there room for growth? Of course, always. But you, your essence, made of those 200 specializations? It makes the world a better, brighter place. So let them shine.

# Chapter 15

## Mothers and Daughters

D ear Athena,

I was so relieved when I learned my first baby was a boy, for several reasons. First, because I had a good relationship with my dad. Second, I had brothers, and I felt that I could figure out dealing with males. (Whether or not that's true isn't the point.)

Third, and weighing more heavily on my heart, was the way I characterized my relationship with my mom. She and I weren't close when I was growing up. Most of my friends weren't close to their moms, either, so I thought this was normal. Our relationship was not intimate; for most of my adolescence, it was slightly strained and distant. Sure, I started appreciating my parents far more once I went off to college. I respected my mom, I knew she loved me, but she wasn't my confidante. She wasn't someone I went to with my troubles, or my relationships. So, the idea of having a daughter was petrifying to me.

Moms get the raw end of the deal, if you ask me. At least, I know that my mom got the raw end of the deal. It's one of the reasons I was nervous to have kids in the first place: you grow this child in your womb — a creature taking over your body, and your body really does stop being yours; it belongs to that baby. When the baby is born, no one can prepare you for the love that you feel, or for the sleep deprivation you experience. No matter how often they tell you, you just can't know what it feels like to go with such little sleep while simultaneously feeding and nursing and caring for and keeping alive a very helpless, very needy infant who literally depends on you for survival. Meanwhile, you're trying to understand what to do, when, and how, and all the while your hormones are surging so much so that your emotional state can range from being elated, floating on the clouds, to feeling despair so deep it seems like you're in a dungeon, or anxiety so uncertain that you're walking a tightrope over an expansive canyon.

Then, as kids age, it's typically the mom who bears the brunt of the daily dos, the tedious, mundane tasks like getting the kids to school, making meals, picking up the house, getting groceries, doing the laundry, picking up the kids, chauffeuring them to activities, ensuring they have done homework, that they're prepared, putting away their stuff, answering a zillion questions, helping them learn manners and practicing kindness, that they're getting dressed... the list is endless.

Most of the time, all this "managing" is met by resistance from children, coupled with sighs of resignation, or arrogance that they've done it already, or straight-up defiance if they haven't. As one meme I recently read (and related to) said, "I love being called the worst person on Earth from someone who depends on me for food, clothing and shelter."

When things don't go their way, kids say it's mom's fault. If they forget something? Mom's fault. If they can't find something? Mom. Food's terrible? Mom. They don't get their tech time? Mom is the worst. Don't get a phone? Mom's SO mean.

I understand this is normal kid behavior, but it still doesn't make it fun. I also remember how awful I was to my mom when I was growing up. Terrible. I actually *was* the worst. My mom and I fought a lot, we argued, and I didn't like her very much, because, well, she was my mom. I often felt criticized by her, like I wasn't doing something the right way. We didn't do fun things together often. Mostly, it was the business of everyday: to-do lists, cleaning up the house, doing school work, setting the table... Sounds a lot like what I do with you and Michael, doesn't it?

My mom and I didn't talk about what was going on in my life. To be fair, I didn't do this with my dad, either.

We weren't close like that; heart-to-heart conversations were virtually non-existent. This may have been due to a generational gap, because my parents were both from an older generation, and I know for certain that my mom did not have these kinds of conversations with her mother.

Regardless, all of those thoughts were swirling in my emotional head when the ultrasound technician said, "it's a girl." All I was thinking was, "Oh, crap. What am I going to do?" I didn't want a distant relationship with you, but I didn't have an example of how to create intimacy with a daughter. I'd have to figure it out... but what if I failed?

After I had you, I couldn't even fathom my love for you. The depth of love I felt for you and your brother was on an entirely different, beyond guttural, level. It could not, *cannot*, be measured. Unless you're a parent, it's difficult to understand. I can't say that people who don't have children don't feel love deeply, I'm certain they do. It's just a love unlike any other love I've felt, so it's difficult to describe.

Even after I felt it, I doubted my own mother had *ever* experienced the kind of love for me that I felt for you. It just seemed impossible, too outlandish to consider, too *much*. Which is untrue, of course. Now that I *am* a mom, I can sense my own mother's love for me, like deep currents in the ocean that quietly sway and spread, making their way upwards and setting the course for the waves above it. She once told me that she wished she understood the importance of skin-to-skin contact with infants back when we were babies. I can see why. There's something intimately bonding about holding your child's naked body to your own, fueling a connection with absolutely nothing between you.

Thankfully, my relationship with your MeeMa is changing. I am learning to honor her (happily, I might add), to enjoy her presence, and to love her just the way she is and the way she isn't. Together, we are learning to have a friendship, she and I, as I hope I'm learning to have one with you, too.

Just last night you were showing me your yearbook from second grade, and in it is a page where you recorded your favorites: animals (puppies and bunnies), songs (Cover Me in Sunshine by Pink), movies, TV shows, what you want to be when you grow up (you said a vet or a teacher, like me) and who your hero was — and you wrote, "Mommy." That one hugged my heart, sweet girl.

I never would have said that about my mom. About ten years after my dad died, I went through a program called The Landmark Forum, and it was during that intense weekend when I realized that I had been resenting my mom for being the one that survived.

What an ugly truth that is to realize, let me tell you. Was I *that* horrible a person that I resented my mom for surviving an accident she wasn't even in? I realized that not only did I resent her, I was avoiding her. I was withholding affection. In those days, when I saw her name pop up on my phone, I usually felt irritated, sent it to voicemail, and ignored it.

The forum leader asked me, "What do you think that has been like for your mom?" I didn't know, so I got humble and asked.

"Mom, I've realized that I've been resenting you since dad died. Not because I wanted you gone, but because I didn't want *him* to be gone. And because I've resented you, I've withheld love and affection from you. What has that been like for you?"

She answered directly, and, in the understatement of the decade, said, "Well, not very good." I could guess, and I tried to express to her, that she probably felt unloved, undervalued, uncared for, and unimportant. What a terrible way for a mother to feel from her child. It would break my heart if, as an adult, you thought so little of me.

I decided then that I wanted to have a relationship with my mom. It would not be the same as what I had with my dad, because they were different people. But, she was the only parent I had left, and she was my mom. I loved her after all, and I knew she'd loved me and given me her best, so I wanted to value her. I *wanted* to know her. After that weekend, when I saw her name pop up on my phone, I answered it. I still do.

This was another huge leap in self-love, believe it or not, because I started to reframe what I had previously viewed as flaws in my character as wounds that had been unhealed. For example, the fact that I wished my dad was alive and that I resented my mom did not make me a bad daughter, it made me a grieving daughter. The fact that I was afraid to have a daughter didn't make me a bad mom, it made me a concerned mom.

Once I started getting curious about my mom, and learning more about her upbringing and how that affected her, my respect for her grew even more. The lack of love she experienced from her mother (who also experienced lack of love, and even abandonment), the constant criticism, verbal abuse, physical abuse and rage she endured — it's evident my mom has done an outstanding job overcoming that and providing as rich a life as possible for her children.

MeeMa's husband, who was a wonderful dad, wasn't the most outwardly affectionate man, and my mom is a toucher. She loves hugs and kisses, and holding hands. I wonder how often she was made to feel special. I'm guessing, not often. I wonder if she ever thought she was worth such a display. I'd venture to say she didn't. The truth is, my mom IS a kind of hero. She was doing the best she could, given her circumstances and the tools she had at the time. She still is, and she is doing a mighty fine job of it. Most of us are doing the best we can, too.

In Steven Pressfield's book "The Warrior Ethos," he describes how the Spartan King Leonidas chose the 300 men who went to the famous battle of Thermopylae (the movie "300" was based on this battle). That whole culture was made of warriors; they were all skilled enough at combat to go. However, in Pressfield's story, the king did not choose the men based on their physical ability or prowess. Instead, the men were chosen based on the characters of the women in their lives — their mothers, wives, and sisters.[25] Why?

Because the leader knew that if those women fell to pieces after losing their men, then so would their society. The women were the keepers, guardians, and protectors of their society, and of each other.

That king knew that women are powerful, far more powerful than we think. Sweet girl, it's time to stop relegating yourself to less than your greatness. No more dismissing yourself, your body, your brain, your needs, or your power.

Can you even imagine what you could accomplish if you *embraced* your full capacity instead of criticizing it? It would be astounding.

Has MeeMa come around to self-love yet? She's on her journey, like all of us. I still hear her being hyper-critical of herself, and I wonder if she sees her unhealed wounds as faults in her character — which they are not. They are, however, her responsibility, just as my wounds are my responsibility, and your wounds are yours. Remember, Athena, that responsibility has nothing to do with blame, or the reason for the wounds. Responsibility relates only to your ability to respond[26] to those wounds, and what you do with them. The more responsibility you take, the more power you have to influence the outcome.

I hope we have many more years with MeeMa in person. If you had told me when I was 16 that 30 years later, when I had two children of my own, that I would want to become the caretaker for my mom and have her live with us, in our home... well, I would've called you flat dab crazy. But it's absolutely true. I cannot wait for that to happen! I hope you get to know her as the beautiful, generous, intelligent woman she is, a human with an incredibly rich history. I believe we'll find a home here in Florida that allows her to move down here with us so that three generations of strong, capable, and loving women can be together, learn from each other, and honor and support one another.

Women are the pillars of our society, sweet girl, and it's time to treat ourselves — and each other — with the reverence that deserves.

# Chapter 16

## Go Your Own Way

Dear Athena,

I could tell you multiple stories of how you've thrown my heart into a panic and set my blood racing. Having children helped me understand the cliché that kids are like your heart walking around outside your body. I often wondered if I'd have a heart attack after some of your escapades. You've always been a girl who does her own thing, and for the most part, I hope that stays with you.

It started in utero, you know, this doing your own thing. Your dad and I had been trying to get pregnant because of my "advanced maternal age." It wasn't working, because I got my period. Since I had earned a cruise through Arbonne, we decided to quit trying, so that I wouldn't be ready to pop while on that cruise.

Sometime later, I was delivering a training in our school district to a few other teachers, all of whom were recent moms, including my co-presenter. We knew each other fairly well, and during the lunch break, I became so bloated I had to unbutton my pants and lie down on the floor.

One of the other moms asked me, "Are you pregnant?"

I confidently answered, "No! I just had my period, and I'm still nursing Michael."

"Are you sure?" another chimed in. "I felt that way a lot when I was pregnant with my daughter."

That got me wondering... *was* I pregnant? Surely not. I did have one pregnancy test left from when I had checked with Michael, so that evening when I got home, I went straight to the bathroom, opened the test and peed on the stick. Before I even finished peeing, two bold blue lines had popped out.

"Huh! Would you look at that!" I thought. "I'm pregnant!"

I showed Ben, obviously, and called my doctor's office. When they asked me when my last period was, I told them it was just a few days ago, so we scheduled our appointment eight weeks from then. The next day, I had a sneaking suspicion that I was farther along than we thought, so I called back and asked if we could bump up the date. When I went into the clinic, they grabbed the ultrasound wand and proceeded to check things out. In case you don't know, very early on in a pregnancy they do an ultrasound vaginally, using a wand-like instrument instead of using the jelly and machine they later use on the outside of the belly.

When this happened with Michael, at that stage the embryo looked like one misshapen glob, so that's what we were expecting. What we saw, however, was a fully formed body, with a large head and four round nubbins — two for arms and two for legs. You looked like a stuffed animal of some kind.

The ultrasound tech, trying to remain calm, exclaimed, "Oh my! I think you're farther along than we thought."

By the end of that visit, I was told I was 16 weeks along and that I could come back in two weeks to find out the gender! You had slipped through the entire first trimester, and then some, completely under the radar. I knew right then you were going to be a force of nature. (By the way, we never did take that cruise, because you can't bring infants under six months old, and you were two months old at that time. For the record, I would way rather have you than go on a one-week cruise.)

I got another glimpse of you doing your thing when my mom treated us to a week at her timeshare in Puerto Vallarta, Mexico. We had eaten dinner at the restaurant closest to the beach, and were enjoying some after dinner conversation. Apparently, you decided the conversation was dull, and it was time to go. Mind you, you were not yet two years old, but you had finished, so you simply started walking away.

I called to you in Spanish, "Athena, adónde vas, chiq-
uita?" ("Where are you going, little one?)

You ignored me, so I called again.  "Chiqui -chi!
¿Adónde vas?" ("Where are you going?")

This time, you continued walking away without looking back, but you *did* acknowledge me — in the univer-
sal "I don't know" gesture, shrugging, and raising your
hands, palms up, above your shoulders as you walked
away.

You didn't know, and didn't care. You were going to
figure it out as you went. We all thought that was funny,
and kind of awesome. I've always respected your ability
to be on your own and be very content. It's admirable,
my love.

It can also be terrifying.

Once, your dad and I decided to spend a weekend
in Seaside, Oregon. We found a hotel that accepted
dogs so that we could bring Hank. It was the very last
hotel on the beach. It was also outdoor, and may not
have been updated to code. To get to our hotel room,
we walked in an open-air hallway, with railings that
were wide enough to get my head through, much less a
child's head and body. The "red alert" button in my mind
was immediately activated and I made a mental note,
and verbal announcement that no kids were allowed
outside without supervision. We were on the fourth
floor, so that was a very important detail to get straight!

The next day, your dad and Michael both had upset tummies, so they didn't feel good. Michael was on the couch watching the TV, and you were next to him. Ben was in the bathroom, and I decided to take Hank outside for a quick walk. I told your dad where I was going through the bathroom door, and off Hank and I went. When I opened the hotel room door 15 minutes later, Ben was sitting on the couch next to Michael where you had been, and you were nowhere to be found.

I asked Ben, "Where's Athena?"

He said, "I thought she was with you."

Surprisingly, I did not yell at Ben or panic. I walked back out the door I had just entered and headed straight to the railing, looking over it with the dreadful feeling I might see your tiny body sprawled on the ground beneath me. Thankfully, I didn't see it. The immediate wave of relief I felt was instantly replaced by panic that you had been abducted, and at that very minute, were being harmed in some way and I might never see you again. It was all I could do *not* to scream in terror.

Hank and I had just come up the stairwell, so I knew you weren't there. I asked Ben to stay with Michael, because Michael wanted to help find you, but I didn't want to worry about two kids disappearing. Thanks to the Brooklyn Nine-Nine episode your dad and I had recently finished watching a few days earlier, I asked myself, "What would Athena want to do? Think like Athena." (In the episode it was "think like Amy," and they found her in the public library.)

You liked pushing buttons, and seeing how things worked, so I thought, "The elevator! Check the elevator." I ran to it, pressed the button, and waited impatiently for it to arrive, and even more impatiently for the door to open, which, like the hotel, was also old and slow-moving. Unsure of where to go once I was in the elevator, I chose the lobby. Again I waited furiously for the door to close, the elevator to descend, and then for the door to open again once it reached the lobby (I felt I could easily have pulled it open far more quickly with my bare hands than it was ever going to open on its own).

As soon as the door *did* start opening, my eyes began scanning the lobby, searching for signs of you. And there you were, being held in the arms of a hotel employee, happily enjoying the attention and interest the employees were giving you. I let out a breath I didn't know I was holding, relief washed over me and I yelled out, "Athena!"

Another guest noticed me, saying, "There's the mom!" as I rushed over to you.

Evidently, someone had found you wandering on the second floor, and I cannot tell you how thankful I am for that person bringing you to the lobby. They tried asking you questions like, "What's your name?" and "Who's your mommy?" but you were too young to speak at that time. (It was shortly after this incident when we started quizzing Michael, and later, you, on your parents' names, their numbers, and where we live.)

My heart was pounding, the adrenaline surge starting to dissipate, and I was vaguely wondering what these people must think of a mom who can't keep up with her own toddler. Mostly, I was struck by three things:

One, you were safe; thank God.

Two, you were so calm and happy the whole time.

Three, how on earth did you open that heavy-*ss hotel door by yourself and get out?

Sweet girl, *you* are the reason I no longer judge people who keep their kids on leashes, or get those hook latches to put up high on doors to lock kids inside. Those were an intensely terrifying few minutes of my life I hope never to repeat.

Looking back on those two instances — both at the beach — you were so nonchalant about them. Granted, you were two, so you had no idea of the horrors that could befall you; you simply went and you trusted. You did you.

You've always been a fascinating combination of independence and tenderness. You have zero problems being on your own, but you've never slept by yourself one night in your entire life. You and Michael have always shared a room, even when we had space for you to have your own. As a child, you slept with me, because you would *not* sleep unless you were physically touching me. I never thought I'd let my child co-sleep with me, but when I had to decide between you sleeping alone or getting my own sleep at night, the choice was easy: SLEEP. You are fierce, but you are cuddly, too.

I recently read a definition of the word magnetism from Bo Eason that struck me: Magnetism is the ability to affect others with the delight that a person takes in him or herself.[27] Magnetism is a quality you have, baby girl. (So does your brother, and I hope you both keep it.)

When we used to take you places as an infant, people would remark at how special you were, about how you had this energy about you, an aura... maybe it was your delight in being you and interacting with the world as a place to be curious, a place to explore and enjoy. This is an admirable quality, and one that, if you keep it, will keep you authentic, and it will also gain trust from others. People will like you not because you want them to, but because you're being yourself.

For most of my life, I showed up wanting to be liked. There's a big difference between being yourself and wanting to be liked. I don't think I even realized this tendency of mine until after I had you. One day I was listening to Brenè Brown (I think it was her book, "The Gifts of Imperfection,") and she was recounting how one time she was so frazzled with what was going on in her life that when she got to an event, she forgot to want to be liked, and instead just showed up as how she was that day. If I'm remembering correctly, she left feeling happier than she had when she arrived, because she had engaged with people from a place of authenticity instead of trying to fit in.[28]

Fitting in is what I have tried to do almost my whole life. Every time I was somewhere new, or with someone I didn't know, or in a new role, my goal was *not* to show up as me. My goal was to figure out what *they* wanted from me — what their expectations were — so that I could meet *those*. Consequently, I was unhappy with myself most of my life, always feeling like I was never measuring up. That's probably because I lived for others instead of myself. I judged myself based on external markers, instead of internal values.

But you, sweet girl, you go your own way.

Thank you for showing me how it's done. Stay true to yourself and your values. Be yourself, and other people will be drawn to you. They will be mesmerized, because they won't know what to do with you. Respect yourself, and they will respect you. If by some chance they don't, remember that's a sign they're on their own journey of self-love, because when we feel secure in ourselves we don't need to criticize or devalue others. You will have your own self-respect, which matters most of all.

Just make sure I know where you are, please. My mama heart can't take any more of your disappearing acts.

# Chapter 17

## Beauty is in the Eye of the Beholder

Dear Athena,

One morning as you were getting ready in the bathroom, I was taking out the braid we had put in the night before. You looked at yourself in the mirror, and simply stated, "I'm so ugly."

I immediately dismissed your comment, saying, "No you aren't! You're beautiful." Of course, you immediately dismissed *that.*

Wanting to prove my point, I went on to describe your cute freckles, your beautiful green eyes, your adorable smile, and your thoughtful heart. I explained how it's what's inside that makes us beautiful, so that, hopefully, you remember: who you are is not your physical appearance.

My response, however, didn't let you sit with your feelings, or consider why you were thinking that way. It didn't validate how you were feeling, or help you know those feelings are normal, or what to do with those emotions.

So the next day in the car, I asked if you remembered that conversation, which you did.

Glancing at you in the rear view mirror, I said, "You know, I've thought I was ugly many times in my life." Your eyes darted up to meet mine in the mirror.

"In fact," I continued, "most people — if not every person in the whole wide world — feels ugly at different points in their lives. When we feel ugly, it's usually triggered by something we saw, or heard, or did. Do you remember what happened right before you said you were ugly last night?"

You replied, "We took out the braid and my hair didn't look right."

"So you thought it would look a certain way, and when we took it out, it didn't look that way?"

You nodded.

"Yeah, I've felt that way, too. It's hard when we have a picture in our mind of what something will look like, and then it doesn't turn out that way."

I'd like to think you felt a little better after that conversation, more validated, or at least more connected to your mama. I mean, we all have expectations of various outcomes, and when they don't meet those expectations? It's a let down. I've felt that way, too, honey. We all have. It's a natural human tendency.

So is feeling ugly. It happens when there's some-thing we want but don't have, like clear skin, silky hair, stronger muscles, more curves, fewer curves, no wrinkles, more success, more money, a shorter body, a faster body... the list goes on. There are many times in our lives we will feel ugly. This is a human emotion (at least I've not heard of animals feeling this way), and it happens to all people, no matter their gender.

Once, in Nicaragua, you were called "cara de rana" ("frog face"), and you were understandably upset. Gia (our dear friend and nanny) and I took different ap-proaches: I talked about how they might be making fun of you because, in fact, you were pretty, but you looked different from them: skin color, hair color, eye color. Maybe they were envious. Gia related to it and shared how she was teased for being shorter than everyone else when she was little. At some point, both of us agreed you could flip the script and say something like, "Thanks, frogs are so cute!!"

Which leads me to the point: frogs are simply frogs. Some people think they're cute (People like me! I collected frog figurines as a girl.), and others think they're gross and slimy.

Your dad can see a car on the road (in fact, he has many times), and whistle his admiration, stating, "Now *that* is a good looking car." I will look over and sometimes agree with him, but many times, I look at the *exact* same car and think, "Meh. It's alright."

This means nothing about the car, does it? No, the car is simply being itself. The fact that Ben thinks it's gorgeous reflects him — it reveals the thoughts and standards that influence *his* opinion. And when I think it's merely okay, it shows *my* preferences.

Art is another great example of beauty being an individual perspective. Countless times I have been to art museums or galleries, seen a certain piece, and felt confused as to how it was ever considered art in the first place. Other pieces touch me so deeply that I stare at them for several minutes, as others pass right on by without slowing.

Other examples are literature and music. Entire genres can be shunned by multitudes of people, while being wholeheartedly extolled by others, simply due to their personal preferences, upbringing, and cultures. Even members of the same family, in the same culture, can vary greatly in their descriptions of beautiful works of art, song, dance, and literature.

Naturally, these various perspectives of beauty apply to human beings, too. We live in the United States, and are heavily influenced by the beauty industry, advertisements, and media outlets. The standard of beauty is not the same globally, and it changes every several years, much like our fashion trends.

Once, when I was leading a mission trip to Mexico, a few girls and I were staying with a host family, and the women of the house, a mom and grandma, were chatting with us. Somehow, we got onto the subject of female bodies. I explained how in college I used to have bigger boobs, a small waist, and slim hips. At the time of the trip, my breasts were smaller (likely due to no longer taking birth control pills), and my waist and hips were closer to the same size, giving me less noticeable curves, and bigger hips than breasts. I implied this was not the progression I wanted — that I'd rather keep my larger breasts and smaller hips. The Matriarch, however, genuinely responded, "Perfecto!", enthusiastically demonstrating the cultural differences in beauty.

The point is, sweet girl, that our outward appearance has very little to do with our beauty (and *nothing* to do with our value). Regardless of culture, most people would agree that kindness, love, and generosity reflect beauty as a person, or make that person admired, well-liked and attractive. We are literally "attracted" to the energy of a person – *it* attracts *us*. This is why your outward appearance is enhanced — or diminished — by the personality traits inside your heart and mind. It's very possible for someone to be "attractive" physically, but ugly on the inside, and then they somehow become less attractive to us overall. The opposite is also true. Someone we may not find physically appealing becomes much more beautiful once we get to know their hearts, passions and inner qualities. Generally speaking, people want to be around other people whose energies they find attractive.

Nonetheless, I understand how powerful the pull of media and culture can be. The noise the media makes as it pressures women to look and be and act in certain ways is deafening. Many times I've wanted to put my hands over my ears, shut my eyes, and say "lalalalalalalala" to drown it out. I can easily get sucked into it, and it takes intentional actions to keep me out of that mire. In the spring of 2000, I moved away from San Diego, California back to Portland, Oregon. Many people thought I was crazy, leaving the land of eternal sunshine for the rainy mist of the Pacific Northwest. The reason I *stated* for moving was because I missed the seasons, which was partially true. More significantly, however, I didn't like who I was becoming in San Diego.

I was still acting from those chameleon tendencies, making choices based on what I thought others wanted from me, not what *I* actually wanted. I made foolish choices as a teacher, a friend, and with men. I felt myself being pulled into the party scene, the superficial scene of what I looked like, what I wore, what I drove. I knew I wouldn't be able to handle it if I stayed.

I have an aversion to the beauty industry in the United States, while at the same time being a consumer of it. I want to rebel, thinking, "Screw you!" — but I still want to look "pretty." Being judged by our appearance is one of my biggest triggers, probably due to my insecurities growing up, so keep that in mind as you read this section. You already know I think it's important to care for our skin, since it's part of our body. I'm a fan of toxin-free skin-care and cosmetics.

What I don't love is that we live in a society and era where women use lash extensions regularly, microblade our eyebrows, inject our lips, get breast augmentations, get liposuction, add hair extensions, and use botox to remove our wrinkles.

Have I used lash extensions? Yes. Did I love them? Yes! Do I have a set of fake lashes I use on very special occasions? Yes!

Have I considered botox, microblading, and breast work? Yes, yes, and yes! In fact, I would probably use Botox myself if I hadn't read multiple times in the fine print that one of the side effects includes ALS/Lou Gehrig's disease. That's an easy and hard pass for me, because taking a chance that I won't be around for *your* future is too important for me to risk. I'd rather have wrinkles.

I don't hate the fact that these procedures and services are available — of course not! They serve valuable purposes for people who need reconstructive surgery, have alopecia, back issues, and more. I know several people who have had cosmetic surgery after losing weight, having kids, accidents, and for their own personal reasons.

What I abhor is this culture of comparing ourselves to a filter. We are somehow forgetting that the vast majority of the pictures we see of people (whether they be models or everyday people in their social media feeds) are filtered. There are zillions of filters on every app, on every camera, to change the appearance of the face in the photo. We're comparing ourselves to pictures that aren't even real! I hate the feeling that somehow we are *less* beautiful, *less* valuable if we don't use these filters. If I let my natural face show, I am disregarded. If I allow my wrinkles to deepen as I age, I am dismissed. If I leave my boobs looking like mildly deflated balloons after nursing you and your brother, I am removed from the "attractive" category. This is one area I personally still struggle with, and I hate it. I hate that I think my boobs are ugly after my pregnancies. Why can't I like them? Because I've grown up in a culture that tells me they're ugly, and its ingrained in me. I detest this because it's teaching girls that aging (and maybe even motherhood) is to be feared, that it makes you ugly and less desirable.

What if it doesn't? What if taking care of yourself and aging gracefully demonstrates a dedication to health that deserves respect? What if I can look at the lines on my face and see the wonderful history of my life: the laughter and tears, the squinting in the sun, the pain and pleasure, and the wisdom I've gained?  What if, instead of surgically lifting or placing implants under my breasts, I celebrate their life-giving abilities as more important than their appearance?  (Or, at the very least, appreciate that my small bras take up much less space in drawers and suitcases than bigger ones do, which is great for traveling!) What if, instead of degrading the soft pooch of my lower belly that has been distended due to diastasis recti during pregnancies, I appreciate the curves it gives me, and let it remind me of my ability to nurture?  Wouldn't that be nice? I'm still working on it.

I don't judge girls and women who use extensions, inject their lips, get boob jobs, or whatever else. After all, I've considered them myself, and had a few. Honestly, I would probably get a breast lift — and I don't like that. I want to love and appreciate my body the way it IS, not the way the media says it's supposed to be, but that is really hard, sweet girl.

I hate that there are legions of women and young girls who feel the need to alter their appearance, to remold themselves to a filter, to some other person's perspective of what a body or face should look like. Sometimes I wonder: are they conforming, hiding, or trying to protect themselves? We have many ways of protecting ourselves from feeling outcast: masks like beauty, clothing, weight, meanness, or behaviors like numbing, vaping, eating, watching TV, and more.  We hate feeling "ugly" so much

that we do what we can to control or change our appearance to *not* be ugly, in hopes that those feelings go away.
What do they think needs hiding?  Who do they think
needs protection from being seen "as is?" Sometimes,
these enhancements don't *enhance* a person's look; they
draw attention to what's not naturally there.

Let's use lash extensions as an example (I'm using this
example because I have used lash extensions myself).
Some of them are lovely, while some are clearly not
natural looking; it's almost as if a fuzzy caterpillar is
napping on each eyelid. What is the point? Perhaps a
wiser question is, "Who is that for?" If a young girl can
honestly say she feels much better about herself *as a
person* with those lash extensions, go for it.  If she can
look at her face and see beauty without those lashes,
then great!  But if those extensions are there to get
noticed, to fit in with the crowd, to mask an insecurity,
to fill a void — those extensions are likely not going to
help.

Perhaps better questions to ask are:

- If we didn't care what people thought, would we
  pay the money for the botox?

- If we lived in another culture, would we deal
  with the anesthesia, trauma and aftercare of
  augmentation surgery?

- If we were surrounded by people who loved us

for who we are, would we take the time to get the extensions put in?

- Are we really doing these things for ourselves, or because we're afraid of how we rank in some invisible pecking order that some outside force (which also capitalizes on these insecurities) set up?

Did you know that in many cultures, women are the matriarchs? When women are no longer able to bear children and go through menopause, they are honored for their wisdom, respected for their rich histories, and considered assets to the community. These women are not worried about their looks, because they understand their worth comes not from their appearance, but from their personhood. They care for their bodies, yes, but they cultivate their hearts and brains also.

They understand the vital power of the feminine, the ability to bring forth life, both literally and figuratively. They understand the female infradian rhythm. In the U.S., we tend to reduce this to one week of menstruation and the "cranky" emotions that come with it. But this cycle is so much more than that, sweet girl. This cycle, which often lasts 25-32 days, involves hormonal fluctuations that regulate ovulation and menstruation. It includes phases of follicular, ovulatory, and luteal stages, influenced by hormones like estrogen and progesterone.

This cycle governs fertility and affects mood, yes, but it also impacts energy levels, metabolism, and various physiological changes throughout the month.

When you understand it and work with it, you can bring forth more strength and life-force. Understanding the female infradian cycle empowers us to embrace our bodies' incredible harmony of biology and physiology. It fosters self-awareness and optimizes productivity and well-being. By honoring our bodies' rhythms, we can synchronize work, exercise, and self-care with our energy levels, enhancing our performance and resilience. We can understand our emotional breadth of knowledge as a key to our potential, rather than a stigma to avoid. Harnessing our innate rhythms enables us to unlock our full potential and thrive as empowered, confident individuals.

Our beauty stems from our ability to be completely exposed, emotionally *and* physically, and still be confident. Our beauty comes from our recognition that we exist, not because of the external shell of our bodies, but because of who we are inside of them. We are beautiful when we are conscious of the fact that we deserve not only to take up the space around us, but to contribute to it — because we know we belong, and we matter — not due to our looks, but to our essence. I mean, let's be real: does the length of my lashes or shape of my butt make any difference for the world or the people in it? No. What does make a difference is who *I am* for the world, how I show up and treat other people.

It's an exquisite, priceless, and far too uncommon day when a woman can stand naked in front of a mirror, without any makeup or add-ons, without sucking in, flexing, or posing, completely and utterly exposed, look at herself and say, "Wow. YOU are freaking amazing."

Has that happened to you lately, sweet girl?

I'm not going to lie and say I do that on a regular basis, but it's happened, twice. Both times were sparked by Mel Robbin's suggestion to genuinely high five yourself in the mirror, and both times brought me to tears. I'm still unsure as to whether those were tears of joy, or tears of sadness I hadn't experienced this sooner. Regardless, those moments were healing, heartening and strengthening.

I've noticed that my body weight seems to naturally fluctuate throughout the year — some months I'm heavier, other months I'm leaner. I'm learning to appreciate that variation. I've discovered I respect the lean times, when my muscles are clearly visible, the strength and efficiency I feel in my body — like I can do anything! I've also noticed I value the softness that comes with more weight, the curves that add cushion and shape. I can honestly say I'm learning to like both versions of my body, and I'm criticizing less and less.

I've thought about the fact that I dye my hair, instead of letting the gray come through. Does that mean I don't love myself? In some ways I can see that argument. I think of myself as more attractive without the gray hair, or I'm afraid of how old I might look if I let the gray grow, or get rid of the highlights. On the other hand, when I do let my hair go gray, I'd like to think I'll be able to love myself *with* the gray hair. It might take a little adjustment, but I hope I can appreciate who I am, with any hair color.

Speaking of hair, the other night, we had another fight about you brushing your hair. You don't like brushing your hair, because it gets tangled and it hurts. I counter with the argument that if you brushed it regularly, it wouldn't hurt so much. You say that's not true, and there we are, at an impasse. You say you want to cut your hair in a pixie cut. I want to support you in that choice, and I will, but what's swimming beneath the surface is the idea that long hair makes a woman beautiful — an archaic belief that I hate is still swimming around in my mind. I worry that kids at school will say you look like a boy, or make fun of you.

But the truth is, hair of any color, any style, or any length has absolutely no bearing on the worth or value of a person. Neither does any aspect of their outward appearance, of course — including eye lashes, face wrinkles, tummy girth or boob size. My message is not to NOT

BEAUTY IS IN THE EYE OF THE BEHOLDER    143

do any of these things. If you want to get a short haircut, let's get you an appointment! If I want to let my hair go gray, or dye it, then I can! If a woman wants to get botox, do it! It needs to be an honest choice for each person, instead of a shield to block feelings that say they are "not good enough" as they are. Are you doing this for yourself, or to fit a mold? It takes a lot of courage to ask yourself that question, sweet girl. It's a personal thing, and only you will know if you can stand in awe of yourself without any masks at all.

I have seen women get more beautiful as they mature. They become more beautiful precisely because they have dropped the mask, armor and shield. They are comfortable in their own skin. They love themselves for who they *are*. They accept themselves the way they are *and* the way they are not. That makes a woman compelling and magnetic — she knows herself, trusts herself, and relies on herself, not on society or anyone else. A woman full of self-acceptance, self-respect, and self-love is a powerful gift to the world. A woman of *any* age is beautiful when she is powerful, and when she stands in that power — because far more important than status, it gives her influence and contribution.

Beauty is in the eye of the beholder, sweet girl, and the beholder is you. Your opinion of yourself is what matters most, which is why I want you to focus on what makes you feel strong, vibrant, and healthy. What makes you come alive? What compels you to act? When you do *those* things, you become something to behold — and it is beautiful.

# PART FOUR:

## Reconstruction

"'i love myself.'
the
quietest.
simplest.
most
powerful.
revolution.
ever."[29]
— Nayyirah Waheed

*"You also have to know what sparks the light in you so that*
*you, in your own way, can illuminate the world."*
-Oprah Winfrey

# Chapter 18

## Close Calls

Dear Athena,

It's easy to be critical of other people, to judge their behaviors, and to think that you would *never* do that — until that thing actually *does* happen to you, or nearly.

For example, I've yelled at my kids (as you know). I've almost hit a bicyclist. I've driven drunk. I've been in car accidents.

One night, I had enjoyed a couple of drinks at a friend's house, and on my way home, a cyclist, wearing all black, crossed the road in front of me and I nearly hit her. It scared me badly. Emotionally, I condemned myself: "Holy sh*t, Elisa! You're a little buzzed, you should *not* be driving, your dad was killed on his bike — you know better than this!"

Simultaneously, I felt a little more grace for the woman who hit my dad; less judgment for the fact that she admitted to having had a drink before she got in her car to go home that afternoon. She probably had a mimosa for the holiday – I know moms who have mimosas at their kids' birthday parties!

It was so dark that night, and the cyclist wearing all black really did make her barely visible – I didn't see her until I was almost upon her. It gave me a newfound understanding of why it's so dang important to wear reflective gear and bright clothing! It also made me think about that moment when Hank was hit on the road. Hank was all black, on a dark night, on a fast, busy road. Whoever hit him probably didn't even see him until it was too late.

Obviously, I was supremely grateful that I had *not* hit that cyclist. It would have been utterly devastating. I was thankful for the moment, however, because it was a lesson that taught me to have more grace, and less criticism of others.

Another example: Recently, I was in my head about something while we were driving home from your gymnastics class. It was late afternoon, and there was still plenty of sunlight, and we were turning left at a stoplight. It was green, and the car in front of me turned exactly where I was going, so I followed suit – and I did not see the SUV coming straight on. When I did, I slowed down, which was a terrible idea, because it kept me *in* the intersection, instead of getting me *out* of it. The other driver laid on her horn, I put my foot on the gas and drove, waving profuse apologies, uttering many "thank yous" to

God for keeping us safe — and all the while you were oblivious in the backseat, reading.

I hadn't seen that car, just like the woman who hit my dad hadn't seen *him*, as he was hidden behind another car. It was possible she had been in her head, just like I was in that moment. Another lesson.

More grace, less criticism.

Before I had children, when I invited other friends who were parents to do something with me, I would be annoyed when they bowed out, saying they couldn't, that it was too much work. I thought, "How hard can it be?"

Then I had kids, and experienced the effort first-hand: 40 minutes of packing, wrangling, dressing, feeding, and harnessing of children for a 20 minute drive, spending 10 minutes finding parking, and then lugging the kids into the location for a 40 minute visit. Once it's over, you drag them and their supplies back to the car, strap them in, dealing with tantrums or fights or requests the whole ride home. It was exhausting.

More grace. Less criticism.

These moments aren't cheerful or entertaining, but they are important, because they demonstrate how fallible we are as humans. We are *all* prone to error, we can *all* be fragile and flawed. These kinds of instances show how, much of the time, our intentions are good — we simply aren't paying attention. We're stuck in our heads or habits.

Self-love and compassion is learning to flex that awareness muscle, to help it grow — to see yourself as both connected to humanity, as well as a unique, never replicated, necessary piece of the entire puzzle. To paraphrase a quote I read once, the fact that you *make* mistakes doesn't mean *you* are a mistake.

To love ourselves, we have to learn to be our own company — not indifferent company, but good company, company that likes hanging out with you, that considers you an equal, a friend. Company that deems you a worthy person, not despite her flaws, but even because of them.

There's a saying, and I don't know who said it: "I've never met a strong person with an easy past." To be strong requires us to persevere and grow resilient. Without mistakes or hardships, we have no impetus to grow, no catalyst for change.

Did you know, sweet girl, that the way to get stronger is to tear down your muscles? I know it sounds strange, but it's true. Every time you feel sore after a workout, it's because you've caused microscopic tears in your muscle tissue, and as the muscle heals, it grows back bigger and stronger. This is an example of what's known as a "hormetic stressor," something that stresses the body, but can also be helpful for it in controlled doses. Other examples include saunas, ice baths, and intermittent fasting.

Perhaps these "close calls" are hormetic stressors for our minds. Nightmares could be, too. Some scientists believe nightmares are a way for our minds to process different possible reactions to various scenarios.[30] Interesting to consider, don't you think? When I look at them that way, I have an even greater appreciation and admiration for our incredible minds, and I want us to keep learning and using them!

There's a beautiful Japanese form of pottery called Kintsugi, which is translated as golden ("kin") and repair ("tsugi"). When there is a crack in the ceramic, they repair it with lacquer and gold, resulting in a beautiful golden seam where the cracks once were. The point is not to erase the cracks, but to see them, to heal them, and make them beautiful.

That's what I hope you learn to do in this life, Athena. That's what I hope you help other people do, too. Recognize our cracks, heal them, and make them golden.

More grace. Less criticism. Of others and ourselves.

# Chapter 19

---

## Attention, Please.

D ear Athena,

Before you could speak, you and I were hanging at the house, doing an activity at the table. I can't tell you what activity it was, because I wasn't fully present. Why not? Because my phone was with me, and I had it open, checking social media.

You, so honest and true, were trying to get my attention, but it wasn't working. What you did next snapped me to attention: you put your hands, palms flat on either side of my face, and physically swiveled my face so that I was looking at you instead of my phone.

I was taken aback, both by your crystal clear communication, and by my own ability to be distracted, even around someone I adored. Here's one thing I've learned, sweet girl: we can have good intentions and still lose our way.

As the saying goes, "the road to hell is paved with good intentions." I always thought that saying was somewhat harsh and unkind, but now I get it. How I interpret that saying is:

Achieving success, or happiness, or any personal goal sounds really straightforward and easy, but in actuality, it requires you getting hyper-focused. It means you remove distractions, and overcome countless obstacles that get in your way. And, for the real kicker, it requires you to measure yourself by *your* values instead of external sources of success, like hits on social media, your weight, your house, or income.

When we measure ourselves by external standards, our lives become unfulfilled, because you will always be trying to measure up to some external factor, which inevitably gets changed along the way. You'll be living in emotional turmoil, even though you're trying your hardest to be good.

Seems unfair, doesn't it?

What you need to understand, and what I finally realized, is that most of our lives are set up to keep us distracted — out of touch with ourselves and our true desires — even in places that are meant to help us. For example:

Schools are often structured to keep kids behaved, following a plan that someone else created for their learning. (As a former teacher, I am not saying teachers are bad. On the contrary, they're amazing. It's supremely challenging to be a teacher, since we expect kids of different cultures, educational backgrounds, personalities, and families to behave the same way, to learn the same thing, and respond similarly to our styles.)

Standardized tests are used to measure how kids rank against each other in knowledge (but, remember, they do not measure a person's potential), and these tests are are often biased. I'll never forget how one of my new students from Africa was faced with a picture of snow skiing and didn't know the name for it. Or a picture of a bear. This remarkably clever and eager student looked at that picture of a bear, scrunched up his face thoughtfully, and came up with an answer. Before responding, he changed his mind. He shook his head, studying it again, and then suggested hopefully: "Hyena?" It was an excellent answer given his origin and background, where bears (and snow) don't exist.

Medical exams measure height, weight, and body mass index, and track them, giving you some number, which can have very little to do with your overall health.

The IQ test is supposed to measure intelligence, but what its original inventor, Alfred Binet, intended for the test was *not* to show intelligence, but areas of progress and growth. He opposed viewing intelligence as a "fixed quantity," calling this view a "brutal pessimism" to oppose,[31] perhaps because these types of tests actually measures skills that have been acquired so far in that person's life, not intelligence. (Scores on intelligence and aptitude tests can change in the summer or school year, with age, or with practice.)

Certainly, there is a purpose to measuring all of these things, and they can be used to inform progress, indicate patterns, or influence positive decisions. However, they can also be used to impose limits, sort and separate people, apply pressure, and to distract you from what really matters.

Our entire culture is filled with distractions designed to keep you from thinking critically, and instead to keep you comparing yourself with everything around you. This constant ranking system creates unhealthy focus, a need for validation or acceptance from others, and increases our fear and anxiety.

These distractions are exacerbated by our psychological tendency to have what's called a "negative bias" — that means, we remember the negative things that happen more easily and often than recalling positive things.

It's no use making ourselves feel bad for remembering the negative stuff — our brains will always remember the bad more than the good. (In fact, I read in a psychology book that there are more English words for negative emotions than positive ones.) Negativity will simply pop up and often be remembered,[32] which is why it's so important to create and cultivate practices that help you counteract it, and instead, refocus your life on what you *want* to see in it.

Have you heard the story of the old man at the train station? There he was, sitting on a bench, when a businessman got off a train and asked the elderly man, "What kind of people will I find here?"

The old man replied, "What kind of people were there in your old town?"

The businessman responded, "A lot of liars, cheats and dishonest people, that's who."

The old man said, "Well, you'll probably find a lot of those people here, too."

The businessman hurriedly walked away with a scowl. Shortly thereafter, a woman disembarked from a different train, approached the elderly man, and asked him, "What kind of people will I find here?"

The old man replied, "What kind of people were there in your old town?"

The woman responded, "A lot of friendly, honest, and hard-working people."

The old man said, "Well, you'll probably find a lot of those people here, too."

You get what you look for in life.

You may have heard the saying, "What you focus on grows." It's true. If you focus on what you *don't* want in your life, you'll find more of it. If you train your brain to focus on what you want in your day, you'll find more of that. This is a skill to cultivate, not an automatic perspective. I often need to refocus myself multiple times in one day!

The distractions and cultural messages that tell us our happiness and fulfillment is somewhere "out there" are outright lies. There is *nothing* outside of you that can bring you happiness, because happiness comes from you living life in alignment with your values — which are inside of you. Happiness isn't about big momentous occasions like a wedding, a promotion, or a vacation. Happiness comes less from intensity of feeling, and more from frequent moments of peace, self-assuredness, and clarity. Moments of relative calm where you sense, "I can do this. I'm okay."

To experience those moments you need to get clear on what your values are, sweet girl. What matters most to you in life? It's important to remember that values are *not* goals — they're not even achievable. Values are more like lanes we choose to drive in, or the direction in which we are headed.

I used to think that family was a value, but it's not — it's the expression of love, the acceptance and belonging that family offers. I used to think that travel was a value, but it's not — it's the idea of trying new things, of being spontaneous, of sometimes getting uncomfortable in a calculated way... turns out, it's the sense of adventure that's important to me. Jim Kwik's discussion on "means" values and "end" values helped me get clear on mine.[33]

My core values are:

- Health

- Love

- Learning

- Adventure

Once I finally figured out my values, it made it easier to do or not do various activities. It was easier to say yes or no, because I use my values as a filter. I ask myself questions based on my values. For instance:

- Will this help me achieve health (mental, physical, spiritual or emotional)?

- Will this show love?

- Will this teach me anything? What could I learn from this?

- Will this push me outside my comfort zone in a safe, healthy way?

If the answer is yes, I strongly consider it. If it's no, it's off the table.

You know what else is off the table now, my beautiful girl? My cell phone.

I now have time limits on those apps that tend to suck me in. I schedule my day in time blocks, so that I know what I'm doing, when — even when I'm making dinner, writing, checking my phone, or being with you and your brother. Because I got clear on my values, and made a plan to pursue things that align with those values, I am free from the distractions and comparisons — at least, much more than I used to be. I'm learning to measure my progress by how far I have come, not how far I still need to go.

Now, I'm free to choose thoughts, actions and behaviors that truly feel good to me and to who I am as a person — and that brings me happiness. There's a saying, "Where your attention goes, your energy flows." It's also true. If you focus on what you lack, or how terrible you are, you'll notice those things. If you focus on your values, your qualities, you'll find those, too.

You won't need to cradle my face to get my attention, anymore, sweet girl.

You've got it.

The question is, do you have your own?

# Chapter 20

## Harvest Time

Dear Athena,

One of your abilities that surprises me is the way you can remember lyrics so easily. This skill was detected early on, by Maestra Laura at Amiguitos, the Spanish Immersion preschool. Any time there was a song involved, you remembered the words. This is not an example, but a little diddy you loved to sing (do you remember?):

"La vaca Lola, la vaca Lola, tiene cabeza, y tiene cola, y hace... muuuu!" (Translation: "Lola the cow, Lola the cow, she has a head, she has a tail, and she goes... mooo!")

Now when we're driving in the car, I'll flip on the radio and you'll start singing along to a song I don't even know the chorus to, and there you are, singing the chorus and verses with gusto. At the dining room table, too. A playlist will come on, and you'll start singing to the song, while Ben and I look at each other wondering, "How does she know this?"

As a girl, I often got the lyrics wrong, as I'm sure many kids do – and I sang them that way for years to come. I sometimes still do – you and Michael like to poke fun at me because I thought the words in a song said "fried rice" when they actually said "red lights."

Singing makes me happy. (So does whistling.) I love singing in the shower, in the car, in the kitchen – and it's especially fun when you get someone like my old housemate Mollye who can harmonize with you. As you know, I love to make up my own lyrics to catchy tunes. An example you know well is, "Everybody potty one more time, potty one more time, potty one more time," sung to the tune of Eddie Murphy's "Party All The Time." It makes my heart swell with joy (and a little pride) when I hear you and Michael doing the same.

When I was twelve, I knew all the lyrics to "I Want Your Sex" by George Michael. Blatantly about sex, wildly popular, and catchy, I loudly sang along without understanding all the context. I'm guessing my mom hated it.

I'm pretty sure you don't understand everything that's implied in song lyrics, but I know you get some of it. After all, you are pretty sharp! One thing you do that I appreciate is comment when you don't like the lyrics of a song – for instance, when it says the "B" word that rhymes with witch. You say matter-of-factly that you wish it were a different word, because the word is used unkindly. I love that heart of yours, and hope you keep it, sweet girl.

One area I want you to practice this type of discernment is on YouTube. We let you watch it, for a while, which is questionable with all the questionable content out there. There are times I heard what you were listening to and demanded you turn it off, or find something educational to watch. Most of the time that happened, I was hearing bullying, whining, or making fun of other people.

Here's why it's important to pay attention to what you're listening to, what you're reading, or what you're watching: because your mind is fertile ground. Very fertile. Once a seed is planted, it takes very little for that seed to take root, sprout, and grow, especially if you hear, read, or see that information again. In fact, repetition is the key to making something automatic. Once you do something often enough, it no longer requires thoughtful attention. This is called "developing automaticity." You've experienced this already through learning to walk, although you don't remember it, with riding your bike, and more recently, tying your shoes. You'll discover it again when you get really good at catching a pop fly in softball, or when you learn to drive. At first it'll seem so hard, but soon enough, you'll arrive at a destination and not remember how you got there!

The point is, you want to plant seeds of the thoughts you *want* your mind to grow. Be intentional about those seeds. Do you want seeds of entitlement, whininess and selfishness, so you can become someone who complains when she doesn't get her way? If so, keep whining. Or, would you rather plant seeds of love, self-care, and generosity, so that you become a person who values other people as much as you value yourself? Then keep practicing patience, kindness and compassion. It takes intentional planting for the second option, unfortunately, because what you find on most entertainment and news outlets is negative-focused, not positive. You're going to have to make this a choice and regularly pull *out* the weeds from the soil of your mind, and put *in* the ones you desire.

One of the many ways I've found to do this is by turning OFF music and screens — by enjoying the silence. The reason I like silence is because it shuts off the noise from external sources, and it allows me to hear the internal noise more clearly. When it's quiet, I can actually hear the messages in my head, and consider if those thoughts are serving me or stopping me. Without the noise, I can choose what seeds I want to plant in my mind, and continue to water them by choosing what to listen to or watch. Then, when it's time for harvest, I'm pleased with the crop, instead of being disgusted or ashamed by it.

Are you ready for me to get a little deeper here? There's a theory circulating that the cells in your body respond to the beliefs in your mind; that in fact, your cells are in constant communication with your mind, acting as if they are tuned to the frequency of each other — which sort of makes your body its own radio channel.

A Japanese researcher named Dr. Masaru Emoto conducted experiments on water molecules. What he did was label water with different messages. Some had positive messages, like "Thank you," "Love and gratitude," and "Harmony" on them. Others had negative messages, like "You disgust me," "Evil," and "You fool" on them.

During the experiment, Dr. Emoto thought those messages, and spoke those messages, over the water for a period of time. Then, he photographed the water crystals to see what effect they had on their structure. The pictures are stunning, actually. The uplifting and encouraging words created beautiful, symmetrical crystals that look a lot like snowflakes. The negative words created crystals that looked empty, scratched, and spongy.

Sounds a little crazy, right? His theory was that our words and thoughts have vibrations attached, and those vibrations physically alter the molecular structure of who or what they are spoken over. He was especially adamant that our words have a profound effect on children — and I know this to be true because I've seen it with you, with my students, and experienced it in my own life.

Regardless of whether or not Dr. Emoto's experiments were valid, I'm guessing most people can agree that words ARE powerful, because we have all heard some words that hit us like a ton of bricks, and other words that comfort us like a healing balm. Words create ideas, and ideas, when they take root in the brain, are powerful and can even overtake the body. This is evidenced in anxiety, panic attacks, depression, and even vertigo or seizures. When parents talk about kids being "shy" in that child's presence, they stay shy. When parents talk about kids being "hard-working," "friendly," and "caring," guess what they become? Hard-working, friendly, and caring.

Words are impactful. Our words and beliefs can actually impact the neurotransmitters of our brains, sweet girl.

How does it happen? I still can't wrap my head around it fully, but the truth is, we are all energy. We are not our bodies. We are not our bellies, our hands, or our heads. We are energy, and energy can neither be created nor destroyed. Energy is and always will be.

How does this energy of our beliefs matter to our lives? Because our beliefs, what we believe in our minds, absolutely affects what our bodies do with that information. If you want to get deeper into this subject, you can check out Dr. Bruce Lipton, a pioneer in the field of epigenetics, the study of what influences our genes.

Dr. Lipton explains that genes themselves do not turn on or off. They cannot do that. Your genes are like the blueprints. They don't actually build the house — they show how it can be built.[34] The contractor is the person who actually builds the house, and the blueprints can change along the way. Guess who is the contractor, and the architect of your body? You are.

Another way to think about genes are like volume knobs and switches. These knobs and switches can be turned up or down, on or off, by things like our environment, nutrition, other genes, hormones, and more. The more we learn, the more we understand that genes aren't responsible for a single trait or specific outcome; they are merely one important player among many that influence how our genes are expressed.[35] (If you'd like to learn more about this topic, I refer you to David Shenk's fascinating book, "The Genius in All of Us.")

Epigenetics is the study of how our environment — and our perception of our environment — impacts our genes. When we teach people that their genes are their destiny, we are teaching people to become victims. Dr. Lipton's work is all about showing how you are actually a *creator* of your life, and of how your genes are expressed. Your words, silent or spoken, shape your life.

This means your thoughts are actively impacting the cells in your body, your potential. Your body has about 50 trillion living cells in it, and they all die and are re-produced regularly. Where do the new cells come from? Your stem cells, which are like blank baby cells that can become any kind of cell. Dr. Lipton explains that you can put identical stem cells in separate Petri dishes, and they will replicate and create more stem cells. Some stem cells will become muscles, others will become bone, and others will become fat. What determines their final product? Not their genes, because they are all from the same parent cell. What determines their outcome is the environment of the Petri dish they live in — their aquarium, if you will. If you change the environment, you can change the end result.

The implications mean that *we* are able to impact the outcome of our genes by the thought environment in which we put them. Your brain chemistry is able to create images in your mind, and if you have a healthy image, then you have healthy chemistry in your cells. If you have a negative image in your mind, then your brain chemistry reflects that negativity, and has an adverse impact on you.

If that sounds kind of far-fetched, sweet girl, consider the placebo effect. The placebo effect is when, in a study, some people get a medication, while other people don't — but they think they are, they're just taking a pill with nothing in it. What happens is the people who *don't* get the real medication experience the *same* healing as the people who *did* take the drug, because they *thought* they were taking the drug — even though they weren't. It was their perception, their *belief,* that the medicine would help, and so it did — even though they weren't taking the actual medicine. It's estimated that over one third of *all* healing in medicine is due to the placebo effect.

Interestingly, they've shown the opposite, too, and it's called the "nocebo effect." This happens when people develop side effects or symptoms after taking a fake drug. The pill they took actually does NOT have any side effects, because it isn't even medicine, but they thought they were taking a real drug, so they started showing symptoms of those side effects the *real* drug might have caused. This is another example of how powerful our thinking can be.

One more example, because it's too crazy not to mention: There is also placebo surgery!  People received fake arthroscopic surgery — the doctors made incisions in a patient's knee, and the patients under general anesthetic could hear doctors talking as if they HAD done it — they even showed video of someone else's knee surgery being done. The *fake* surgery had the *same* effect as the *actual* surgery, where they drained fluid and scraped cartilage, but the surgery *never even happened.*

Obviously, your *belief* about what is happening *in* you or *to* you makes an impact. This is really important to understand, Athena. This makes a HUGE difference in how much you enjoy your life. If we can look at what happens to us and make it mean something positive, we have a much better chance of being happy and fulfilled. Every single thing that happens is simply an event – there is no meaning or value in that event, except for the significance we create for it, and the value we give it.

Let's get back to the idea of your body being a radio station. Your body is tuned to the frequency of you, and all your cells are listening. My radio station is called "Elisa." Your radio station is named "Athena."

The cells in your bodies have antennas on their surface to receive signals, just like TV antennas. They are made of proteins. No two people have the same antennas. Even though all your cells have different jobs, they are all listening to the same station, and that is your mind. All the cells in your body have the antennas to hear your frequency, and that's because if your mind senses an emergency, like an earthquake, ALL your cells need to hear you and cooperate in order to survive.

Well, it turns out that if I put my cells in someone else's body, they're receiving a different broadcast and won't listen without intervention. Here are a few examples of this:

Dr. Lipton explains how people have actually done readings of the electrical activity of cells from one person, and moved those cells up to 40 miles away. When they make the one person feel an emotional response, the cells 40 miles away activate their electrical activity .[36] That means cells can still respond to your frequency, even when they aren't in your body. Isn't that amazing?

Another example is heart transplants. During a heart transplant, the people receiving the organ are given medication that shuts down their immune system, so that their body won't attack the newly transplanted organ (this process is true for any organ transplant). Once the heart transplant is established, those medications are gradually decreased, which lets the new heart get used to its new surroundings.  It has been documented that the new owner can "pick up" characteristics of the original heart owner. This is called Cellular Memory Transfer. A light-hearted example is when a woman who was a vegetarian received a new heart, and she suddenly developed a taste for beer and chicken McNuggets. Apparently, those were favorite foods of the donor.

A more serious example was the story of a young girl who received a heart from another young child. Soon after, she began having frequent nightmares of being murdered. Every time, she dreamt the same scene and the same murder. So, the doctors traced the history of the donor, and sure enough, the donor was a little girl who was killed. As a result, the police spoke with the recipient, and they were actually able to catch the killer based on her description of her nightmare.

This still gives me chills thinking about it! The cells in our bodies are literally communicating with each other. They are listening to our minds, our thoughts, and acting accordingly.

The implications of these findings are tremendous, don't you think? The thoughts you have — both conscious or subconscious — are actively influencing your life. If you change your thoughts, you can literally change your life. As David Shenk explained, "Every day in every way you are helping to shape which genes become active."[37]

Your body is listening to YOU, honey love. If you want to change your health, or your personality, or how people treat you, you must not say things like, "I'm too tired." "I'm too young (or old, if you're a mama)." "It's too late." "It's too soon." "I'm too busy." "It's just the way it is." None of that is true, it's simply the truth you are currently repeating to yourself.

The reality is, you are *powerful*, sweet girl. Even *now*, even this very *day*, you are, and have been, influencing your health and the quality of your life. The question is, *how*? Are your thoughts influencing your life for the positive, or negative? Pay attention to those thoughts, and make them count.

# Chapter 21

## Batting Averages

Dear Athena,

One day as I was driving on 33rd Avenue in Portland, I drove through a school zone. Parents were picking up their kids, and one mom, who was carrying her young daughter, caught my eye. The mom had her daughter hitched up on her left hip, her right hand cupping her daughter's face. She was looking at her daughter intently, and the delight and love she felt for her daughter was evident, flowing freely, pouring into her child. Her daughter was beaming, looking back at her mom, and the moment struck me as so intimate that I felt I needed to look away, that I shouldn't be witnessing such tenderness. It was mesmerizing, and I didn't *want* to look away; in fact, I kept them in view through the rear view mirror of my car until they fell out of sight. This was back when I was still single, before I even met your dad.

Now, I have those moments with you and your brother. Moments where I look at you in wonder and awe, disbelieving how lucky I am that I get to call you mine, that *I* get to be *your* mom. Those times are precious to me, because it's so easy to get caught up in the daily schedule, to get frustrated, and forget how magnificent it really is.

Sometimes, I see glimpses of you both as grown adults. They are so fleeting they are difficult to explain, streaking across they sky of my mind in a split second like a meteor. They're impossible to hold onto long enough to see clearly, but just long enough to get an idea of who you will become, or what you will look like. They're lightning flashes into a future portal, blips on a screen, gone before you have a chance to register what you just saw.

I love those moments, because I am stunned by you young people, how incredible you both are, how fully you are *already* your own people, yet still will change significantly. I'm astonished by how much you teach me.

It's that last one that's the hardest, because being a mom — or really a parent, I should say — confronts you with every single flaw you see in yourself, and others you don't. When things are rough, they are genuinely tough, and it's easy to get sucked into old habits and behaviors you find unappealing, like yelling and adult temper tantrums (yes, they happen), snide criticism, or biting sarcasm.

When things are smooth, you feel like you're getting the hang of it, that you might be figuring this whole parenthood thing out — and then, all of a sudden, even though the same thing has happened before without negative consequence, one of you kids will explode, or take it the wrong way, or misinterpret it — and you're back where you started.

For example, just last night, after watching a movie, we turned off the TV and asked you to go brush your teeth. We often brush our teeth together, and when I said you could go start without me, your face immediately downcast. I followed you into the bathroom, and you were sitting on the toilet, crying into your hands.

"You don't care about me anymore!" you sobbed.

"Why would you think that, honey?"

"You've told me to brush my teeth without you three days in a row!"

Sometimes, like in that instance, I'll see how the event or statement could be misinterpreted, and we'll be able to talk about it, me validating your feelings, and then explaining what I actually meant. Other times, you'll repeat back what you think you heard me say and it's exactly *not* what I said, which can either leave me completely flabbergasted, wondering how to proceed, or degenerate into an argument about who's right or who's wrong.

Many days, I will stay calm during the arguments about screen time after school. I'll maintain composure when you complain about the food I prepare or serve for dinner. I'll restrain myself as you bicker and scream at each other, *after* I've asked you repeatedly not to do whatever it is that was aggravating the other, like keeping your hands off of each other, not screaming, speaking with love, no name calling, etc. I'll be patient when you delay bedtime for the umpteenth time... and then, I'll snap when you jump on the bed that last time, or throw the Nerf football and accidentally hit me with it.

When I lose it, I yell. Is it any wonder why you two yell when you're mad? You see me do it. I hate it when I yell, because it's loud and angry, and I don't want to be that mom who yells. So when I do, I'm very good at belittling myself:

"See that, Elisa? You've yelled at your kids again. At bedtime, no less, so the last memory they have of you is your ugly, scrunched up face, scolding them in anger. Here you are, thinking you're such a good mom. Pshaw. You suck! And your kids know it."

Down I go into a shame spiral, feeling like maybe I should've never had kids, that I'm no good, that I'm scarring you both for life. I start thinking you're never going to have friends because of my yelling, and sometimes, when it's very strong, I'll think, maybe you'd be better off without me. To be clear, I would *never* hurt myself, and I don't want to die — I actually want to live as long as possible. I'm saying these because it's important to show you how shame can truly mess with your mind, and cause you to consider options that aren't *ever* helpful, and even harmful. But sometimes, when I'm in a shame spiral, I wonder if I *did* die, if I *did* leave, *would* you be better off?  Which is a brazen and audacious *lie*, but a very powerful one nonetheless. (I repeat, here and now, to make sure you've heard me: I will *never* leave you of my own volition.)

This is why telling someone that you're in a shame spiral is absolutely critical, my love. When you recognize that you are shaming yourself, and getting deeper into it, it is *vital* that you call or text someone. You don't need to give them details; it can be as quick as saying, "Hey, I'm in a shame spiral and I need to talk to someone." The reason you actually *do* need to talk to someone, even if you don't feel like it, even if you're mortified of your behavior, is because shame grows when it's kept secret, and it begins to disappear when you speak it.

I don't recommend telling everyone, by the way, only people who love you and who have earned a place for you to be vulnerable and authentic. These are usually people who are trustworthy, vulnerable, and authentic themselves. These people will call you or respond as soon as possible to your request, and when they do, they will listen. They will not show surprise at what you've done (*Wow! You?? I can't believe it!*), or dismay (*No! You didn't!*), or diminish it (*It's no big deal. It could be worse.*)

No, these people will listen and say, "That feeling really sucks. It's happened to me, too." And then they'll talk about it with you, as much or as little as you want.

I have two people I call when I'm in a shame spiral. One of them is my dear friend Kim H., and one of them is your dad. They both understand parenting shame, because they've experienced it themselves. I'm grateful your dad gets it, since he's the person I see every night when I go to sleep and every day when I wake up. Thankfully, he and I don't often have bad days simultaneously, so if one of us is having an off day, the other one can be with you kids and let the other person be the way they are, without judgment.

Often, your dad will remind me of who I really am: a loving, caring mom. He'll also remind me that perfection is unattainable, and actually, doesn't even exist. He'll even throw in a sports analogy, like batting averages. On the days I lose it, I've already been up to bat several times. I may have gotten a base hit, a run batted in, a foul ball, a triple. Many times I'll walk, and then that one time I do strike out, I strike out swinging hard.

Let's say I went up to bat five times that day, was successful four times and struck out once — that's an 80% batting average, .800, which is absolutely phenomenal, considering most professional baseball players have batting averages around .300. This is overly simplified, I know, but it's helpful to remember, because our failures

— our strikeouts — loom very large in our minds, and we can be fooled into thinking that they define us. They do not.

What *does* define us is how we reorient ourselves to who we really are, how we adjust our attitude and stance to hit the ball the way we want to, no matter which way it's thrown next time, and what we do with what follows the hit.

So, my sweet, strong, and sassy girl, be warned: you will not dodge that shady shame character. It's shifty, and it'll find you, and try to drag you under. When it does, reach out to someone you can trust: me, your daddy, a dear friend; someone who will shine the light on shame. Once it's no longer shrouded in darkness, it won't feel quite so scary. Remember, there is nothing you can do that would make me love you less, nothing that will make you less valuable, nothing that will make you unworthy... and anything that tells you otherwise is a lying shadow that needs to be exposed. Turn your face to the sun so you can see the light, baby girl, and see yourself clearly.

# Chapter 22

---

## Food Junkie

Dear Athena,

When you were a toddler, and just starting to eat solid foods, I would always love to see your reaction. This was true of Michael, too, because kids' expressions are so, well... expressive.

But you were *vocal* about your food, especially foods you liked. You would taste and remark, not with words, but with sounds: saying "Mmmmmm," or smacking your lips in pleasure. You'd also react with movements, like clapping your chubby hands enthusiastically, or your entire face would radiate surprise and delight.

That's my girl.

My friend Stef saw you one day and exclaimed, "She's like us, Lis!" She was right. You are my food-motivated child, and you take after your mom.

When I was about your age — a little older, maybe 9 or 10, I still sucked my thumb at night. My dad had tried multiple tricks to stop me, including putting hot sauce on it, but I was content with sucking my right thumb, which I had deemed my chocolate thumb (vanilla was my left thumb, so it remained untouched).

None of his other strategies worked, but he finally landed on one that did: he told me that for every night I *didn't* suck my thumb, he would treat me to an ice cream cone from Baskin-Robbins. Let me tell you, every night from then on, before I'd go to bed, I'd look at my right thumb in determination, shove it under my pillow, and plaster my cheek against the pillow, face down, so that I wouldn't be tempted. Guess what? It worked! (Can you guess which of the 31 flavors I usually got? Hint: it wasn't vanilla.)

I never tried that on you, because all the experts say we shouldn't make food a reward (which I actually agree with), but we already do, and it already is, so maybe I should've tried it.

I worry that you and Michael will revolt against eating healthfully because your dad and I are so focused on it, sort of like children of pastors who walk away from religion, and get into drugs and wild lifestyles. The other argument is that the apple doesn't fall far from the tree, so if we raise you in a certain way, chances are, you will turn out behaving similarly. I guess we'll have to wait and see, right?

I love food, sweet girl, I really do. I love eating it — a lot of it. I love savory foods, with herbs and spices. I love sweet foods, like cookies, muffins, cakes, and pies. I love curries, stir fries, and sauces. I love multiple cuisines: Thai, Indian, Italian, Korean, Greek, Mexican, Ethiopian. I love vegetables of many kinds. I love fruits and citrus. I love chocolate, but not milk or white. I love melted, gooey things like chocolate fondue, cheese, or slightly under-baked brownies. I love planning meals, preparing food, going out for food, gifting food, talking about food, and shopping for food. In fact, I much prefer grocery shopping over shopping for clothes or gifts. I love smelling, savoring, and devouring food. Most of my happiest memories involve food. If something tastes good, I want more of it. I often want to eat it until there's no more left, or until I'm so uncomfortable that I can't eat anymore.

I've had to learn to control myself — not only with food, but in my emotions, too. I've only been able to do this with practice, awareness, and perspective.

One of the traps I used to fall into was believing that food was good or bad; that healthy foods were "good," and unhealthy foods were "bad." I took this to mean that if I ate healthy foods, the good foods, then I was *being* good — I was a good person. When I ate the unhealthy foods, the bad foods, then I was *being* bad — a bad person. The reason this is a problem is because it makes food a moral issue, which it most certainly is *not*. Food is a matter of survival, of being able to thrive. When we consider foods as good or bad, there is an implication that a person who eats healthier foods than you is "better" than you, which in turn implies that if you are eating healthier foods than someone else, it makes *you* a better person than *that* person. The whole concept is outrageous and misleading.

I see this kind of trickery everywhere: when people claim they had a "cheat" meal, or they were "so bad" on vacation, or say things like, "I'm not as good as you are," or "You're so good with your food," or even the common practice of putting food into "good" or "bad" categories.

The other problem with viewing food as good or bad is that the "bad" foods become off limits, as if you can never have them. And what happens when you can't have it? You want it more, of course.

This is connected to the second trap of viewing food with a "scarcity" mindset, one that I can still fall into easily. If you think you can't have something, your brain automatically wants it more, and it leads to more binging of that thing. We can look at underage drinking in the United States versus underage drinking in other countries as one piece of evidence for this. Here in the U.S., where we label drinking as "bad" until you are 21, then somehow, magically it is okay, teens (and adults, too) often drink simply to get drunk, which frequently leads to negative consequences. In other countries, however, where drinking ages are lower, and where there's not as much of a negative stigma attached, teenagers and young adults drink to enjoy much more than to get drunk. If you're never allowed to eat ice cream, you'll eat much more than you need in one sitting, because you don't know when you're going to get to eat it again.

This scarcity mindset can also manifest as not wanting to waste anything. I can remember my grandma, Mum Jane, lecturing me to finish the food on my plate with her slight southern drawl, "Child, I lived through the depression!"

I grew up believing that I had to finish what was on my plate, even if I was full. We were taught not to waste anything — so leftovers stayed in the fridge and we ate them, until they were gone. Each week we had at least one "leftover night," where we'd reheat everything left in the fridge and help ourselves.

Every once in a while, MeeMa would put a new spin on the leftovers, and create a new recipe. Most of the time, these were tasty, since she was a good cook. However, when we lived in Guam, she once made a casserole made up of leftovers, using our leftover pancakes as part of it. My brothers and I served ourselves, as was the expectation, and took hesitant bites. It was terrible, but we didn't say anything; we just waited until my dad took his first bite.

He did, and when we heard the words, "Good god, this is awful!" we sighed with relief. We ended up giving it to the dogs outside, and even they wouldn't eat it!

Regardless of that one snafu, leftover night was always fun — we could pick and choose which leftovers we wanted to eat.

I still do my best to eat up leftovers. I like making double batches of recipes, because it not only lets me spend fewer nights a week cooking (saving time), but it also gives me lunches throughout the week, as well as future meals when I freeze them. That food philosophy was ingrained in me well. I hate wasting food.

However, sometimes it's okay for food to be tossed.

One of the best pieces of advice I got (from an ex-boyfriend, by the way) was this: "The food is going to go to waste somewhere: either in your body or in the garbage. Why would you want it going to waste in your body?" I mean, he had a point. It's much easier for the plate to get rid of waste than it is your body. I remember that advice when I'm tempted to stuff myself too full, or overindulge in brownies. I freely practice it after Halloween, and every Christmas when I toss the leftover Christmas cookies, and it feels great.

It's a smart question to consider. Where *is* the food going to waste? Instead of viewing food as something I "can't" have, I practice healthier habits like eating until I'm satisfied, not stuffed, and saying to myself, "I CAN have dessert whenever I want, I simply choose to eat it infrequently." (I do not count the small squares of dark chocolate I eat after dinner as an indulgent dessert.)

While it's completely true that certain foods hold more nutritional value than other foods, that doesn't make food good or bad. It's simply food. Food is not something you earn by exercising, or having a rough day. It's a basic need for survival. You must have food to survive. In order for your body and brain to truly thrive, you need foods that are high in nutritional value, often.[3839]

That's what I want for you, sweet girl: to thrive. I want you to give your beautiful, incredible body the food it needs to go out there and crush it everyday, food that keeps that incredible, limitless brain of yours that you use so well, firing fast and curiously, food that enables you to pursue a plethora of activities until you figure out which ones make your heart and spirit come alive, and food that then lets you do those things, as frequently and as unabashedly as you choose.

This doesn't mean you will never overeat on brownies hot out of the oven, or have too many warm cookies with a little raw cookie dough on top, slightly melted (thank you to my old roommate Mollye for this bit of goodness; if you've not tried it, you might want to; you're welcome), or an entire batch of homemade Rice Krispie treats, or a whole bag of Doritos, or two bowls of ice cream or too many slices of pizza — all of which I've personally done, by the way.

No, this means you practice *being* with your food, really tasting and enjoying it, even talking about how much you enjoy a certain aspect of it. It means savoring it, identifying and appreciating individual flavors within it, along with the texture and aroma. It means considering all the people that helped you eat what you're enjoying now, and being grateful for them: the farmers who planted the seed, the harvesters that collected it, the drivers that carried it to the store, the shelvers who arranged it so beautifully, and the person who prepared it for you — whether that is you or someone else. Being present with your food is learning that you don't have to eat it all now, that you can and will have it again, which means you can enjoy some now, and more later, if you feel like it (which you may or may not feel like doing). It means you think about how food makes you feel, and the reasons you're eating it. Do you actually want it, or are you mindlessly eating out of habit or emotion?

It means loving your body, and your taste buds, enough to know that your body truly *does* need those nutrient-dense foods to work best, so you honor it by giving it those foods daily. It means incorporating a variety of fresh fruits and vegetables often, focusing on how frequently you eat nourishing foods, and also how often you are enjoying the rich foods that, while they taste incredibly satisfying, usually become toxic if eaten too frequently, or in too large of doses.

I appreciate Dr. Daniel Amen's analogy: Imagine you had a prized racehorse. Would you ever feed it junk food?

Would you ever let it sit for days without training? Aren't you worth more than a race horse?[40] Now, if you just answered that question in your mind with something like, "Well, as a matter of fact, I'm *not* worth as much as a race horse. *I'm* not making millions of dollars running any races." You're not alone. I used to think that, too. But you ARE worth more than that horse. *Far* more, and you don't have to sprint to prove it.

This practice of being intentional and mindful about your food is not always easy, and that's okay. There are many times I've wanted to say, "Forget this! It's not worth it. I just want to eat cookies and pizza all day."

But then I remember *why* I want to eat mindfully: because my brain is the only one I have; my body is the only vehicle I have to experience this life, and this life is where *you* are, Athena, where your brother and your dad are, and all the other people I love. It's where I can see colors, enjoy nature, feel the wind on my face, and hear music — and I want to extend my time in this lifetime as long as I possibly can. I want to be around for the people in your life that *you* end up loving. I want to respect and honor my brain and body so that I can be fully functioning and able-bodied, so that I can sit with, stand beside, walk among, and play alongside these beautiful souls that get to be in your world, who get to be loved by you.

I know that my food and lifestyle choices are *the* most important keys for that vision to come to fruition. That desire to be present in your life for as long as possible makes all my food choices worthwhile — and it makes an adventure of it, too.

What's your vision for life, sweet girl? Decades into the future, what do you see for yourself? I hope it's a life of vitality, passion, and joy. Remember: the food you eat and the lifestyle you keep are important factors that will either lead you towards that vision, or away from it. It's in your hands to make it happen.

# Chapter 23

---

# The Comparison Trap

Dear Athena,

Recently you were invited to a pool party. When you went to put on your swimsuit, we quickly discovered you had outgrown all of yours. Thankfully, you had some shorts and a shirt you could wear.

Soon after, we went bathing suit shopping, which, you'll likely discover later, most women don't enjoy. All my years growing up, I knew I was supposed to be skinny. That's what all the photos showed. Well, you are not a skinny girl. You are tall, thick, and sturdy. Your belly is rounded. Thankfully, more photos are reflecting different body shapes in bathing suits these days, but the dominant image of "attractive" in the media is still someone thin and lanky. That's one of the problems of society's messages to women — they change. It's infuriating because women are constantly trying to measure up to media images that are rarely constant, not based on anything substantial, and continually morphing. If you measure yourself against these images, it almost guarantees a life of feeling "less than."

Back to the story. You and I went to Target, and, as an 8-year old, grabbed all the large and extra large bathing suits that were there, since I wasn't sure which size would fit you better. I was wondering how it would go, because I had all *my* history being in bathing suits playing through my head.

We chose a fitting room and went inside. My job was to take the bathing suits off the hangers and hand them to you, and you'd decide if they were yeses, maybes, or nos. You loved all of them, and were excited to try them on — the crop tops, the one-pieces, the bikinis. But I worried, how would you react when you saw them on your body?

I passed you the first one-piece. "Ooooh, I love it!"

I passed you the second one-piece. "This is so pretty!"

I passed you the crop top, and before you even tried it on, you blew me away with your prediction: "This is going to look sooooo beautiful on me!"

With every suit, you struck a pose. You smiled at your reflection. Even when you rubbed your belly.

My heartbeat slowed down and my breath calmed. I think I can speak for the majority of women when I say that it was so shocking —yet *refreshing*— to hear a girl say she looked *good* in a bathing suit. I hope it's not the last time I hear that from you, because you are beautiful in any bathing suit you choose to wear — or even none at all.

Nevertheless, we need to talk about this topic of comparison, sweet girl. It's a big one, because there will probably never be a day that you don't somehow compare yourself to another person, or against yourself: how you *used* to be, or against some ideal you have in your head about how you're *supposed* to be.

Ugh! I really hate this one, because it wreaks so much havoc in our lives. I read a quote once that said, "All unhappiness is caused by comparison," and I suspect it's true. It's hard to know how to even tackle this topic, because there's so much to it: a natural human tendency, hedonic adaptation, envy, jealousy — and likely more than I understand. Where do I start?

I'll start with myself, since I'm the expert on myself and know myself the best — just like you are the expert on you, and don't let anyone tell you otherwise. By the way, this doesn't mean you don't have room to grow, or things to learn; we all do. It simply means you know what's going on inside your mind and body better than anyone, since you are the one experiencing it.

Ever since I can remember, I've been comparing myself to others:

- "Maybe if I were prettier, George and Helen would have let me be Queen one day."

- "Maybe if I acted rebellious like Winnie, I would

be popular."

- "If I were smart like my brother, math would have been easy."

- "If I were creative like Ava, I'd be such a better teacher."

- "Maybe I need a better sense of humor. I should crack more jokes, like Ophelia."

- "You'd think that after doing CrossFit for over ten years, I'd be stronger by now. Look at her, she's only been doing it for 2 years and she's already competing at levels I never will."

- "If I were more entertaining like those people, I would have more followers on social media."

- "If I were just more organized like Julie, I wouldn't have these problems."

- "If I were better at crafts/more patient/more fun, I'd be a better mom."

You see? It's never ending, and in all areas of life.

What gets more complicated is that I *know* comparison is usually detrimental, especially when there's a touch of shame or self-degradation involved, so I beat myself up for comparing.

- "I shouldn't be comparing myself to her — we're totally different ages and different stages of life."

- "If only I compared myself less, then I'd be happier. I shouldn't compare myself to others."

- "There you go again, Elisa, looking at other people with envy."

Do you see the irony? I'm shaming myself for feeling shame, another thing we humans are really good at doing, especially moms.

Comparing is a natural human tendency; we all do it. We get used to what we've got, so we want something new or different; we begin to take it for granted. Comparison isn't always bad, either; it can be a sign of admiration or respect. More often than not, however, it's used to rank ourselves against some invisible system, and that is detrimental. For instance, who says how many followers a person should have? Who says how funny a person needs to be? Who says rebellious people are more popular? These are invisible ranking systems, where someone is ranked higher than you are, and maybe there is someone lower than you. All these ranking systems do is categorize people; they rate people by some system that doesn't even exist, instead of considering the person as a whole and simply letting them exist, as they are.

What has helped me is acknowledging how human it is for us to compare — of *course* we do it. There's nothing wrong with me, or you, or anyone else, for making comparisons. It has also helped me to understand the difference between envy and jealousy, and how to reframe them.

Envy and jealousy often get misused, or used as synonyms, although they are distinct. As always, I appreciate Brenè Brown's explanations.[41]

Envy is what we feel when we want something another person has. It usually involves two people, and happens when one person doesn't have what the other person has. Some examples could be (and these are all taken from my life): she has a great boyfriend, she is so strong, she has a successful business, what a huge following she has, she is so talented.

Often, but not always, envy comes with a feeling of hostility. You might feel angry because they have it and you don't. You might experience thoughts like, "Why shouldn't I have that, too?" "I want that and I don't want her to have it." Or, "If I can't have it, I don't want *her* to have it, either."

Jealousy, on the other hand, is not wanting something we don't have, it's a fear of *losing* a relationship or part of a relationship we *already* have. It usually happens in response to fear, anger, or sadness. Jealousy usually involves three people — two people in a relationship and an outside force, which is usually a person, but it could be an activity that threatens the partnership. Examples: In a relationship, one person is unfaithful to the other with a third person; one of the people in a relationship takes up a new activity, or gets a new job that takes up much more time, so the other person is left feeling lonely or left out. It could even be a new child, like an older sibling who could be jealous of the time the new baby gets with the parents.

Usually, when we compare ourselves to others, or at least when I do it, it's because I'm *envious* of something that they have that I want. It's not usually jealousy, though I've experienced that plenty of times in my life. These are common states of mind that all humans experience at various times throughout their lives.

If we learn to reframe these natural tendencies, we can stop making ourselves out to be terrible people, when we're really just being human, and then we can start making forward progress.

I appreciate Mel Robbins' take on envy and jealousy: she says they're an indicator of a desire that you have that's been blocked, a sign of something you crave.[42] So, instead of dismissing it, or saying that it's wrong, pay attention to it and decide if it's something you really want. If it is, work towards it — just because someone else has it doesn't mean you can't also. If, after explor-ing that desire, you determine it's not a priority, then you can appreciate it and set it aside. You can, and will, change priorities many times throughout your life.

When I first read this in Mel's book, "The High Five Habit," I realized I had been envious of a colleague of mine who had several things I wanted: a promotion, a beautiful home, patience with her children, and more. I reached out to her and told her all of this, because it was actually a form of admiration, and proof that if she could do it, I could, too. Ironically, she said she thought the same of *my* business!

The other concept that has helped me get a grip on comparison is understanding hedonic adaptation — which is a fancy way of saying that when life is good, we eventually get used to it being that way, and then it takes *more* for us to feel as good, and we start becoming dissatisfied with what *used* to satisfy us.

Isn't it crazy the tricks that our minds play on us? Apparently, hedonic adaptation has an evolutionary pur-pose: eons ago, if we got too comfortable, we would fail to grow, get lethargic, or even die, which I suppose could have been true. These days, however, it does cause some trouble when we stop being satisfied with two drinks, or two cookies, so we start having three or four, or if we get an iPhone, and then see the newest version and think that one is better, or think that only shoes costing upwards of $200 are acceptable, and so forth.

The problem with all of this, sweet girl, is that we are looking for something outside of ourselves to make us happy: two more cookies, a new phone, 10 more pounds that we either want to lose or lift. When we look *outside* of ourselves to solve a problem that's *inside* of us, we will never find a solution. We will always feel dissatisfied, unhappy, or unfulfilled.

Now, when I find myself comparing, I get brave and look a little deeper - what insecurity is lurking there?

If only I could lift more / do more / achieve more — those thoughts reveal my insecurity that I am not good enough as I am, that I need to prove myself, or make my existence worth something. Once I recognize that insecurity at work in my thoughts, I can remind myself of my values and keep staying in my lane.

Being envious of another person's success shows that I want and crave success for myself — I don't mind that they have it, I just want it, too. So, I can ask myself what success looks like to me, and what steps I can take to get there.

Looking at others and thinking, she's so fast / pretty / strong / smart / successful — those kinds of thoughts again reveal my insecurity that I am not enough, that people will like or respect others more than they respect or like me. Even if it's someone I admire, this can be hard, because you want the best for them, but wish you had it, too.

In these cases, it really is on you to take control of your mind, to name what is happening. I actually say out loud things like, "I see you, amazing lady," or, "I see you, envy, and I recognize that I want that too. I can only control me. I don't have your life or your circumstances, your mind, or your body. I have mine, and I'm learning to respect and honor it." When I find myself in the middle of a negative comparison, I call it out, and do my best to wish them well on their day and then focus on mine.

Your dad is the one who taught me that it's okay to let yourself sit with your feelings, even the ones you don't like very much. When you feel grumpy or grouchy, that's okay. It doesn't mean anything is wrong. It means something is bugging you.

We don't normally let ourselves be with emotions that are labeled as "negative," like anger, shame, sadness, envy, disappointment, or vulnerability. Why not? Because it's uncomfortable to sit with them. Nevertheless, it's an important skill to learn. As your mom, it's hard for me to see you in those emotions. I know how terrible it feels, and I want to rescue you. However, if I try to distract you from them ("*How about we paint our toenails together?*"), or dismiss your thoughts of feeling "less than" someone else ("*Honey, you are just as smart and clever and pretty as she is!*"), you'll never be able to get yourself through it. Even though the reason I'm doing it is to save you from the discomfort you're feeling, it's not helping you grow.

Of *course* you will always have me on your side; I've always got your back. I *do* think you're incredible, I'm so *proud* to be your mom, and I'm so happy *you* are my daughter. That's all 100% true. But, the only way you will learn to love yourself and have your own back is if you learn to recognize your own humanity, to talk *yourself* off the ledge, to remind yourself that those moments of feeling "less than" happen to all of us, and, most importantly, that those feelings are *not* fact.

Our feelings change. One minute we can feel hopeful; the next hopeless. We didn't change, our feelings did. Something triggered that change. While our feelings are valid, they are also fleeting. I learned from Dr. Joan Rosenburg that most of our emotions come in waves of 90 seconds, so if you can ride those waves, you'll be more able to handle them.[43] I have told your daddy many times that feelings are fickle creatures designed to deceive us. (It can be annoying when he then repeats this back to me when I say things like, "I feel like a fraud!") We must learn to acknowledge our feelings and look for the trigger, the underlying insecurity, and then address *that*.

Your emotions are powerful, sweet girl. Let them be there, and be present with them; consider where they're coming from. Remember what Dr. Caroline Leaf says about emotions: there's nothing wrong with them. They don't mean anything is wrong with you. They show areas that are in need of healing and growth.[44] When we resist these feelings, we don't give ourselves the chance, or the freedom, to even begin the process of healing. Resisting negative emotions often looks like:

- ignoring them by dismissing them, thinking they're silly or not as bad as someone else's struggles

- judging them by criticizing ourselves for feeling them at all, saying we should be "over" this by now, or we're "better" than this

- hiding or burying them by not talking about them, covering them up under busy schedules, shopping, or other activities

- overworking or overexercising ourselves so we are too tired to deal with them

- numbing them with food, alcohol, vaping, sex, or drug use

- escaping them by entertaining ourselves with TV, video games, or social media

Despite our best efforts to avoid them, the only thing these distractions succeed in doing is allowing our emotions to slowly simmer on a back burner. We fool ourselves when we think we're over them. When we resist these emotions, they persist. They'll keep showing up in our lives.

However, if we accept our feelings, get curious about them, and choose to look at them, then we can contemplate *ourselves*. We can lovingly wonder *why* we are feeling this way. Self-compassion allows us to be open to understanding our shared humanity, to consider other possibilities for growth, and expand our ability to impact ourselves and the world around us.

The bottom line is, when we resist, we keep ourselves small and confined within a certain scope we imagine to be our reality. When we accept the way we really are, we break down the walls of that imaginary box, and are able to find ways to step outside of it.

You're going to compare and feel insecure multiple times throughout your life, sweet girl. Do your best to remember that *everyone* is feeling insecure about something, and even comparing themselves, too. It's no use focusing on them. They have to do that for themselves. Focus on you. Your emotions are not the enemy; they are allies. They are your clues as to what you need to deal with in your life. They might be uncomfortable, but you can handle them, and you need to. Remember: There's nowhere to arrive. You *are* the destination.

# Chapter 24

---

# Be On Your Own Team

Dear Athena,

When you were nearly five, we went and visited Uncle Chris, Aunt Marvelliz, and MeeMa in Seattle — I believe it was the very first visit to his new house. We went to a park down the road that's attached to a school, where, as long as recess isn't in session, the public can use it. It has all sorts of fun things to do: the spinning mushroom, the tower tent of ropes, the monkey bars, music, play structures, and more. Two of the climbing structures are connected by a loose net made of ropes and knots.

You were on one of the structures, and wanted to get to the other one via the rope net, but it was scary! It had big holes you could easily fall through, it was elevated, and it swayed when you climbed on it. I was keeping an eye on you, because as your mom, I wanted you to explore, but I also didn't want you to hurt yourself.

At one point, you looked hesitant, unsure of what to do, or where to place your feet and hands. I noticed your lips moving, so I inched closer without distracting you, so I could hear what you were saying. Your words made my heart swell with pride. You were repeating to yourself, "You can do it! You've got this!"

That, my girl, is an example of being on your own team — and it's a critical component of you staying true to yourself, as well as to your success.

I wish I could say we keep this quality as we age, but we don't. We begin noticing differences between ourselves and others, we start comparing, and then the stories in our heads sprout up, saying we need to change, do something different, or be another way in order to be okay or accepted.

Soon enough, the words coming out of our mouths are "I'm stupid," "I'm ugly," "I can't get this!" All of which I've said to myself many times over the years, and which I've heard you say already, which saddens my heart deeply. Eventually, we all learn that saying these kinds of phrases *out loud* isn't accepted in polite company, so we keep them quiet... but those voices continue to sound inside of our heads.

There's a comment I've read and repeated several times: if you wouldn't say it to the person you love the most, it's not something to tell yourself, either. This is actually a barometer of sorts I have used for myself.

When I think something negative about myself, I ask, "Would I say this to Michael or Athena?" If not, then it's not something I'm going to listen to, either. I mean, think about it — if you were to say those things to your best friend, how long would she be your friend? "Mary, you're stupid! You're ugly! You're never going to get this!"

Mary wouldn't be your friend for very long, right? Can you even imagine?

The thing is, sweet girl, every time we say those things about ourselves, we are making it harder and harder to not only like ourselves, but to *trust* ourselves, and be happy with our lives. When we focus so much on the ways we don't measure up, we get bitter, resentful, and angry. We complain more, we throw tantrums, we play the victim. We say things aren't fair, or they're too hard, so we eventually give up. We end up living mediocre lives, never reaching our potential, never stepping into our greatness, or our message for the world. We settle.

One of the definitions of "settle" is to slowly sink to the bottom. Can you see that picture? You sinking to the bottom, letting everything around you move on, or float up, or catch a current elsewhere. Meanwhile, you stay stuck and unmoving at the bottom, eventually running out of air. I don't want that for you.

No one teaches you how to be on your own team, though. No one teaches you, and maybe it's because no one realizes that if you're always criticizing yourself, or always comparing yourself to the future you haven't had yet, you'll never arrive — because once you get to one point, the place you're supposed to be has changed.

I should know, because I did it for 44 years. It wasn't until that bathtub moment with you and Michael that I discovered I needed to be on my own team. I also realized I had no idea how to do it, but I was determined to learn — for your sakes and mine.

I'm really fortunate and grateful to have your daddy as my partner, because I *know* he's on my team. In fact, I use that phrase a lot when I describe him to other people. I know he's on my team, because he encourages me to play up, and assures me that there's nothing wrong when I feel down. He works *with* me in parenting, housework, and finances, towards goals that we set together. He practices with me, he performs with me. Sometimes he plays while I rest; other days I play while he rests. He even rearranges his schedule for me when I need him to, and he does this without complaining. He listens to my needs, and does his best to meet them, without getting defensive. He shares his needs with me, and I try to meet them. He calls me out when I'm not being a team player, and I'm getting better at admitting my faults without getting defensive, and seeing my behavior from his (valid) point of view. He and I have done a lot of work *together* to make it this far, by the way. It didn't happen easily, or naturally. The natural inclination was to walk away from each other thinking we were right and they were wrong, to hole up inside ourselves and avoid conflict, and then resent the other person. Let me tell you, the continued work to be a team is worth it.

On the other hand, your dad and I are not codependent on each other. I know that if I didn't have him, I'd be okay, because I've learned how to support myself. He knows the same thing about himself. We don't *need* each other, we just really enjoy each other, and *choose* each other, every single day. It took time, focus, and effort for us to grow and change, as individuals *and* as a couple. It required taking classes where we learned techniques and strategies to examine ourselves, how to communicate clearly, and, most importantly: listen attentively — with the intention of understanding, not making a point. We had to make our team a priority.

The same is true for you, being on your own team. You have to make *you* a priority. This is not to say that you will not have trusted friends and beautiful relationships. You can, will, and need those people in your life — no one can do life alone, at least not very well, or for very long. I hope you find a partner who, like your dad, is willing to invest in themselves and your relationship. Regardless, *you* have to learn to be on your own team, just like I had to learn to do it, too. After all, your friends may change. Your partner might not always be around.

You have to learn how to have your own back, sweet girl. You've got to come through for yourself, because in reality, you're the only one who can.

For me, part of this meant removing the word "against" from my vocabulary when talking about myself. Have you heard the concept of "you're not in competition with anyone else; you're only competing against yourself"? It's pretty common these days, especially in the wellness world. I'm all about continual growth and progress, but I don't love that idea, or at least the way it's phrased. I understand what it means, but to me that expression immediately raises an "Us vs. Them" mentality. It invokes comparison, and even if it's against myself, that means I'm on the other side — that I'm not on the same team, that I'm no longer my own partner — that I've been pitted *against* myself.

That personally puts me in a negative headspace, so instead, my focus is on moving with my body *beyond* where I am now, whether that be at the gym, as a parent, or a daughter. And guess what, sweet girl: here's something I rarely hear, but it's true nonetheless: you can choose to stay where you are in one area if you like where you are. *You* get to decide which areas are worthy of exerting the effort to grow or change, and no one else.

For instance, I'm consciously still working on my patience as a mom, and my communication as a daughter. I've still got goals at the gym, like getting my double unders (that's when the jump rope goes under your feet twice in one jump), and after that, handstand walks. I *don't* have goals in nutrition, because that has been a focus of mine for years now, and I feel both confident and competent in that area. I'm also aware that all of this could change at any time, depending on my stage of life and circumstances. When I need to adjust, I will.

I'm practicing living in a "gain" mindset, instead of a "gap" mindset, a great tip I picked up from Benjamin Hardy and Dan Sullivan.[1] I practice being grateful for what I have, and focus on the progress I'm making, instead of how far I still want to go. For example, I used to focus on how I couldn't do double unders anymore, even though I used to be able to do them before I had children. That's a gap mentality. A gain mentality is celebrating the sixteen double unders that I strung together today, which is many more than I could have done four months ago. Or, instead of shaming myself for losing my temper in the car after school on Friday and thinking "Ugh! I suck!", I intentionally reframe that and remember, "I was able to keep my cool 4 out of 5 days in the car this week. That's improvement."

Here's the thing: I can't make you happy. Your daddy can't make you happy. Neither can Michael, your best friend, or anyone you love. Your achievements won't make you happy either, especially if you think they'll give you success.

The only person that can make you happy is *you*, by becoming your own partner and enjoying life. The way you do that is multifaceted. In my experience it requires three components:

First, you need to know who you want to be, decades from now — I'm talking 20, 30, 40 or even 50 years from today. You need to know who you will be, what you want to be able to do, and how you want to be living. That's your identity. You tell yourself a story about who you want to be, and who you are, and start living into that identity. I tell myself I'm a healthy, loving, active woman who can independently travel and learn long into my 80s and beyond.

Second, you need to value your vessel. You need to show your body the respect and care it deserves through food, exercise, sleep, and stress management. I can't expect my 80-year-old body to be able to jump, twist, or walk if I don't do those things now. I can't expect my muscles, brain, and heart to sustain themselves then if I don't care for them now.

Three, you need to stay in your lane. You need to know the core values and ideals that are important to you, and then live in alignment with them. You need to create standards to live by, using those values and your future identity. I can't expect to be a healthy, loving, and active 80 year-old unless I focus on doing the things that help me get there today, and avoid doing the things that won't.

Being on your own team will require you to guard your mind, train it and use it to your advantage. Remember, your intelligence, skills, and personality are not fixed. They develop as they interact with our environment, situations, and nutrition. To paraphrase author David Shenk, we have the extraordinary power to change our own circumstances and lift our individual performance,[45] be that mental, emotional or physical. It will be obvious to other people that you are on your own team because they'll be able to see your actions, words, and behaviors and know what you're working towards. Happiness in life often comes from us staying in touch with what we want for our lives — which requires us to *know* what we want — and trusting ourselves that we can act in alignment with that desire. This is important, because your future will not necessarily become what you *want* it to be, it will become who you are *being*. If what you *want* and who you are *being* match, the probability is higher you will achieve that vision. If they don't, chances are much, much lower.

There are entire books, courses, and fields of study devoted to all of these things, and maybe one day I'll get to add to that collection. In the meantime, however, just know that you can do it. You *can* be who you want to be in 20 or 30 or 40 years. You *can* figure out your values. You *can* manage your own mind. You *can* live in alignment. You *can* treat your body well and enjoy life simultaneously. You *can* be on your own team. It won't happen by accident, but it can happen on purpose — and it will — if you learn to be your own partner.

I read a quote once that said, "Love does not consist of two people looking at each other, but looking forward in the same direction." That's what I feel like we need to do with ourselves, sweet girl. We've been against ourselves for so long, that we need to consider our bodies and minds as two beings, and join forces, so that we can look forward, together, and move united towards that future. That's what being on your team means. Be your own partner, Athena, and you'll be unstoppable.

# Chapter 25

---

# Yellow Bleeping

D ear Athena,
  This spring was your first time playing softball, a new sport you've never played, with new people you don't know. I was so proud of your courage, going even though you were nervous and a little afraid of being the rookie. You did a great job, too! Batting, throwing, and catching — you did it all! Granted, you were a little timid, but that's to be expected when something is new or unfamiliar.

The only problem was that your practices were on Mondays and Wednesdays — which means you couldn't do gymnastics on Mondays anymore, and you couldn't do Wednesdays because of theater class. I couldn't even take you after theater was over, because practice ran at exactly the same time. To make it more complicated, once games started, Monday practices turned into Monday games, so the only time you'd have to practice was on Wednesday — which you couldn't make. This means you'd

only be going to the fields for games. There's nothing in-
herently wrong with this, but to me, practices are where
you try new skills, get coaching, and have a safe space to
make mistakes. A game is a much different environment,
because the focus is on winning, rather than learning.

My mama-bear heart raised its head in concern, because, since you've never played before, I worried this
might make the whole experience less fun for you. You
might not grow in skills, or develop the relationships
with teammates as much as you would if you were able
to go to practices. Part of me wanted to use this as
a way to model managing disappointments, to let you
have a less-than-ideal experience. That would be a good
learning opportunity.

The other part of me wanted to fight for you. I figured
there wasn't much to be done — switching teams wasn't
an option, as that would displace another family — but
I reached out to another mom and softball coordinator
anyway. I expressed my concerns (nicely, I hope), and
asked what the options were. I was fully anticipating
an answer of "nothing," so when the actual response
explained that the other team's coach would be happy to
have you practice with their team on Thursday nights, I
was genuinely surprised — and touched by her generosity
of spirit.

I was so glad I asked. If you never ask, the answer is
always going to be "no," right? I know you've heard me

say that, because just yesterday I heard *you* say those exact words to our neighbor when you asked if you could go to her house for a while.

This is what we call "advocacy," the act of gathering support for a cause or person. Speaking up for yourself, speaking your truth and needs, is part of self-advocacy, and learning that skill is critical for you to be on your own team and live a life you love. Without it, you will often be dismissed, perhaps unintentionally, but it'll happen nevertheless. Your needs and feelings will go unaddressed unless you learn to advocate for yourself.

Why don't more people do this? Perhaps because advocacy can be uncomfortable. For example, on our way home from that first softball practice, you were saying it wasn't fun, because your friend, the only friend you knew at the time, "flicked" you when you were trying to play with her. You felt dismissed and were upset about that. I suggested you tell her how you felt, saying something like, "I didn't feel good when you flicked me. Were you trying to tell me something?" You immediately shut down that idea. I understand why, sweet girl.

Saying something like that is vulnerable. It puts you in a space of possible rejection or ridicule. You might be angry, frustrated, or disappointed because the vision you had in your mind of how it was going to go didn't play out. If you speak up, you might hear something you don't want to hear, something unkind or hurtful.

On the other hand, you might hear something positive you weren't expecting, or a perspective you hadn't
considered. When you advocate for yourself, it gives the
other person a chance to play up, to be a more inclusive
or more articulate person. (For example, they might surprise you by letting you practice with them on Thursday
nights.)

They might also be inspired by your example of speaking up for yourself, sweet girl. Perhaps they don't know
self-advocacy is even a possibility, and your example
empowers them to consider that they might speak up
for themselves one day. They might hear your words and
think, "Wow, she is powerful and brave because she sticks
up for herself," and then they might think they could be
that way, too.

You already know how to do this, by the way. When
Michael was around four, he was playing soccer for the
first time, and we were at one of his games. It was half
time, so you and a few other kids were playing around
with one of the balls on the field while the boys were
meeting. When the coach yelled, "Time!", you started
making your way to the sideline with the ball. One of the
boys on the other team, wearing a #2 jersey, came over
to you and took the ball from you. Your face scrunched
up, your brow furrowed, and your almost three-year-old
self pointed a finger straight at his chest and yelled, "NO,
two!" That is self-advocacy at its very core. I was so proud

of you for sticking up for yourself at such a young age, knowing intrinsically that your truth was valid and worth acknowledging.

You know when else you self-advocated? After the games started in softball. The other team you practiced with was a younger team, which was a little strange, but it was more so once you started competing against them. It simply didn't feel right to you to keep practicing with them. As your mom, I was tempted to force you to keep practicing so you could get the skills. But to what end? So we could fight about going to practice each week? That wouldn't be fun for either of us, and would likely end in you resenting both me and softball. When I asked if you'd like to go to games only, and you said yes, that was you telling me what you needed — simply to go to the games and be with your team. I'm glad I listened to you, sweet girl. If you didn't learn or improve, so be it (but you did). More importantly, you'd be playing a sport in a way you enjoyed, and making friends in the process. Even more important than that was that you saw your needs fulfilled, instead of overlooked. It's important to trust yourself, honey, and honor those intuitions.

Your daddy makes Michael practice self-advocacy, too. He makes him do research and calls on his own. Remember when Michael got interested in playing pool (billiards)? He wanted your daddy to take him to a pool hall, which he said he would, as long as Michael did the research to find out where he could go, age requirements, and cost. Michael went to work, googling billiard halls near us, finding their phone numbers, and calling them to ask questions he couldn't find answers to on their websites.

When Daddy finally took him to one, Michael approached a woman working at the bar and asked where they went to start playing, or some question like that. The woman said, "Are you the kid that called?" Michael hadn't spoken to her, but whoever did told her all about the young boy who had called with inquiring questions. When you advocate for yourself, people take notice.

Self-advocacy also means setting boundaries, and knowing what your limits are. Your brother actually helped me find an easy way to tell you two when I was nearing the edge of my limits. Do you remember those laser guns he got for his birthday? They start with a green light, and when you're out of "life," it turns to red. When you're getting low, it turns to yellow. When you're really low, and in danger of dying, the yellow light starts flashing on and off.

One night when I was putting you to bed, I was getting impatient, and Michael declared, "Mom! You're yellow bleeping!" It took me a minute to figure out that he was referring to the very low light on those guns, but when I got it, I said, "Yes! That's exactly right! I *am* yellow bleeping." I had been dangerously low on energy and was about to lose it. Knowing that, and communicating that in a way you kids understood, helped not only lighten the mood, but also seemed to make you more cooperative. You seemed to get it. Now I can say to you all, "I'm yellow bleeping," and you know what that means.

Even when you know your limits, there are times you will have to advocate for yourself after you've done something you're not proud of, by the way. Many times, I'm guessing. I've gotten much better at this since becoming a parent, because I've done countless things I wish I hadn't, and I've had to repair the damage. I'm forever grateful for Dr. Becky Kennedy's book "Good Inside" that has helped me do this effectively, and without shaming myself. Even if you're *not* a parent, you will inevitably mess up with friends, lovers, coworkers, or random acquaintances. And when you do, self-advocacy will be important for maintaining the relationship.

A time I'm remembering now is when I took you and Michael to get a free personal pizza with the coupons you got from making the Honor Roll. You had gotten a coupon for a smoothie, and Michael for pizza, and he asked if we could go get it that very day. I chose to be spontaneous and said, "Sure!" Once we were there, I got you a pizza also, since we could use your smoothie coupon another time.

Well, Michael got very upset, because in his mind he had earned the *pizza*, and you didn't, and complained that I was getting you one also, so much so that by the time he got his pizza, he didn't even want it anymore. At that point, I quickly lost it and started yelling about how ungrateful he was, and how they are just coupons and no one is deciding which kid gets which coupon, they just shove them in the envelopes with the report cards, and by the way, I didn't even *have* to take you to get pizza at ALL. Then someone slammed on the brakes in front of me, so I slammed on mine, and the pizza went flying. There was complaining about how it fell on the floor, and then I was really screaming about how I was just going to throw that effing pizza away!  By the time we got home, *everyone* was in a foul mood... and not much pizza was eaten.

I had gone straight from green to yellow to yellow bleeping to red in the blink of an eye, faster than I could recognize and contain.  I was ready to start spinning down a shame cycle about what a terrible parent I was. The thing is, I was so proud of myself for even being open to taking you to get the pizza after school in the first place, instead of sticking to our regular routine — and then it all blew up in my face.

Once I collected myself, I went back to you and Michael and apologized. "I'm so sorry for yelling at you, honeys. Mommy got really frustrated, and instead of staying calm, I lost my patience, and then I was embarrassed by my yelling. Plus, I got really scared when we almost got in an accident, which made me even more edgy, so I ended up yelling more. I know that wasn't fun to hear or feel, and I'm sorry."

There are many other times I break the connection between us, and every time I try and go back and repair it. I know I can't remove the rupture, but hopefully, I can explain myself enough to patch it. Your mommy is still a work in progress and I try to show you that I realize that, and even still, in my state of imperfection, I'm worthy of your trust and love. As I learned from Dr. Becky, our goal isn't to be perfect, it's to get really, *really* good at repair.[46] Not only with others, but with yourself, too. That's also self-advocacy.

This may not seem important, sweet girl, but it is. You need to know when you feel green, red, or yellow bleeping. Communicate your needs. Listen to other peoples' needs, too. If you don't speak up for yourself, someone else will speak for you. Take it from me, that doesn't feel good. It doesn't work out well, either, because what ends up happening is that *you* start sitting in the backseat of your *own* car, and letting other people drive where *they* want to go, without regard for you and what you need. Your voice matters. Speak your voice, Athena, even if it cracks.

# Chapter 26

---

# Everything Always Works Out For Us

D ear Athena,
　　Your dad and I have told you and Michael our family motto a few times, and it's worth repeating: Everything always works out for us.

This is our family mantra. Your dad started it, and we've adopted it, because it's true. Life always works out the way it does. That doesn't mean it's easy, or painless, or even fair. It means we are responsible for our parts to play, for how we respond to what happens, and for what we do with what life gives us.

When your leg was broken by the boy that ran into you on his bike, I didn't have health care, because I wasn't employed with enough hours to have it, and it happened in the week before I would have those hours, having just accepted an additional role in the school district. Instead of freaking out, I explained it to my Superintendent at work, and he backdated my hire date so that I would have insurance. Bless him, because that relieved incredible financial stress from our shoulders. Life works out for us because we make the most of it. Instead of whining or blaming, we say, "Okay. Here's the situation. Now what? What are the options?"

Having this perspective really empowers you, sweet girl. It empowers you to find a solution, to be a problem solver — just like you already are. Remember the Halloween we were making holes in the pumpkin so that we could fill them with peanut butter and put it out for the squirrels to carve the rest? You were having trouble pushing the hole cutter into the pumpkin, and instead of getting frustrated you looked around, saw the jar of peanut butter, and used it as a hammer — very effectively, I might add. That's what I'm talking about!

Being a problem solver enables you to be a creator in life, rather than a victim — and that leads to self-confidence, because you know you can rely on yourself to figure something out and get through it. There's no need to get the next step *right*, because A), there's no such thing, and B), if you don't like the way things are headed, you can simply change your course. That's living in power.

Another way to stay in power is to watch your tone of voice. Is it one of a bystander, or one of a change agent? Here's what I mean.

Last Sunday, you and our neighbor girl were playing outside, and her brother came up, took your water bottle, and threw it under the car. In retaliation, you filled his shoes with dirt and water, and then chose to peel paint off of the stairwell. The boy came and told on you (although he did not explain the part about the water bottle), and we sent you to your room for a little while. When we came and talked with you, we asked what you wanted to tell us. That's when you told us about the water bottle, in a very whiny voice. We've talked to you about your whiny voice before, because it's not fun to listen to, and more important than that, it makes you a victim — it takes away your power — which, as your mom, is supremely frustrating to watch.

You are *powerful*, sweet girl, everyone around you can see that! Your name, Athena, goddess of war and wisdom, is perfect for you. We named you that for a reason. When you whine and complain, you become someone else. That day, I tried explaining how whining is not how powerful people handle a situation.

We asked you what you thought we were upset about, and when you said filling his shoes with mud, we corrected you — we were actually upset about the act of vandalism, peeling the paint. That does not show respect to another person's property, which is not who we are, because we act from love. Besides, that didn't affect the boy one bit. We have no problem with you sticking up for yourself. You need to learn to do that, because you will need to do that many times in your life — however, you need to learn how to stand your ground effectively and powerfully.

Right now, you are in The Lion King Kids production, and you were chosen to play the part of Mufasa — king of the animals, noble and true. You were chosen for that part because the directors knew you had what it takes to play a powerful role with integrity.

Your daddy had the great idea to ask you if Mufasa would whine if he asked Scar not to do something. "Scar, don't dooooo that!" in a whiny, high-pitched voice.

Would Scar take Mufasa seriously? Absolutely not. He would laugh and dismiss him. But if Mufasa said it in his calm, assured voice: "Scar, don't do that." Would Scar mess with him? Unlikely.

Mufasa knew when to pick a fight and when to walk away. He knew his power, and when he needed to use it. You need to learn the same thing.

Your daddy actually practiced this with you, which was smart and even fun. He told you, "Okay!  Say the the words 'I am powerful,' but say them in your whiniest voice." And you did!  Both of you laughed at how silly it sounded.  I was chuckling in the room next door.

Then he requested, "Now say, 'I am powerful' in your most excited voice!"  And you did, sounding very ener-gized.

Next, he said, "Now try saying it in your laziest voice. You did, very apathetically.

Lastly, he requested, "Now I want you to say it in your strongest voice."

You boldly proclaimed, "I am powerful!" I could hear the change in your demeanor from the timbre of your voice.

Finally, your dad asked you an important question: "Which voice sounds most like you? Which did you like the most?"

Do you remember which voice you chose, sweet girl? The strongest voice. That's not surprising, because you *are* strong; you're a force, remember? That's who you are.

And you know what? So am I. So are all women, though we've been conditioned to stay quiet, to serve others, and to put ourselves last on the totem pole. I'm calling "Poppycock!" on that. Mufasa wouldn't put himself last (and neither would his partner, Sarabi). The only reason he'd do that is if it were to save his son. Otherwise, he would put his most powerful self first, because he knew that's what his pride needed. They needed his *power*, not his fear. They needed his *stability*, not his insecurity. They needed his *assertiveness*, not his whininess. He got *out* of victim mode. He got out of his head and put himself out *there*, among his pride, his people, so to speak.

What did *they* need? How would he raise up the next generation of powerful leaders? Not by letting them sulk or whine, that's for sure. He did it by teaching them who they really were, and expecting them to live into that identity. That's what we have to do, too. You and I need to stand as creators of our lives and be the strongest, most powerful versions of ourselves so that we can lift up the people around us to do the same — because as we lift ourselves up, we also lift them. There's even a quote to describe this: "A rising tide lifts all boats."

No one becomes great by playing small or whining about what other people do to them. It does not show yourself love to play the victim, either. It belittles you, sweet girl. It makes you smaller than you are. You show yourself love, and you become great. You stay in power by responding with intention and respect to your conditions; by searching for, and creating, opportunities and environments that foster love and growth. Be like Mufasa, Athena. You *are* him. And as you do, everything will always work out for you.

# Chapter 27

## Body Beautiful

D ear Athena,
  Yesterday was the first day of CrossFit Kids at Westchase, and you and Michael were the only kids in the class. Even though you were hoping there would be more kids there, we framed that positively, saying how appropriate that you are from the Portland, Oregon area, since the basketball team there is named the Trailblazers.

That's what you two have had to be for the last two years — kids of parents blazing a nomadic trail, including a road trip across 30 states of the country and 18 national parks, a 5-month stay in Nicaragua, a 2-month trip to Italy and France, another 6-month stay in Nicaragua, and house surfing between grandparents' homes in between trips.

When we moved to Florida a little over a year ago, you were the new kids — *again*. And so was I. It was interesting joining different gyms, which is one of the only ways I meet people these days. Since I work from home, and go to bed early, there aren't many people besides other school moms (and a few dads) that I see. I've noticed that very few people say "hello." Even fewer show an interest in you as a new person. It's not easy being new, because you feel conspicuous and ignored simultaneously.

I remember one night while we were eating dinner as a family, I commented to you and Michael, "When there is a new kid at school, I'd like you two to be the ones to say hello and introduce yourselves, because you know how that feels." I explained my reasoning by saying that most people are stuck in their own heads, not considering how it feels to be new or different — which after being the only white, English-speaking kids in the entire Nicaraguan school you attended, you can relate to that, too.

When I was in 9th grade, my dad was stationed in Coronado, California, and I was the new girl *again*, this being my sixth new school in nine years. I can remember only one person taking an interest in me, intentionally befriending me, and that was Kimmy. She made me feel special, and I have loved her ever since.

The point is, most people don't know how to make friends; they don't know what to say to new people. It's quite simple, actually. All it takes is curiosity. Any kind of question will do:

- Where did you move from?

- How do you like it here so far?

- What's it like where you came from?

- Do you have a family / pets / siblings?

Any question that shows interest in them as a person, and who they are, will help break the ice and help them feel welcome.

Here in Florida, I've been the person to say hi, and to ask people about themselves. I've had a lot of practice at it, too, trying five different gyms in one year. I've learned that if I don't talk to people, they don't talk to me, so I'm going to talk! And you know what? I recently got a card from a woman I met at the gym I go to now, thanking me for saying hello — because if I hadn't, she might not have returned. Is it easy for me to say hello when I don't know those people? No, but it gets easier each time I do. Plus, it makes people feel valuable. If I have a chance to make someone feel seen, I'm going to do it.

I've come to believe — or at least I'm wondering — if the people who *are* curious, if the people that *do* take an interest in others, are somehow secure enough in themselves to *not* be stuck in their heads all the time, to get out of worrying what other people are thinking about *them*, and instead, focus on the new person in front of them, and who *they* are. Maybe they have that magnetism of being so sure of themselves that other people enjoy being around them. They're secure in who they are, so they're able to draw others in. I think that's beautiful. I'd love to become that kind of person.

Back to CrossFit. I love that you're trying this, sweet girl. Michael is naturally active — he's moving and sprinting all day long; he already considers himself an athlete. You are more like me — you're content chilling on the couch with a good book, crafting, listening to music, or just being still. It's not that you don't like movement, you're simply as content relaxing as you are moving.

It was so fun watching you learn the deadlift, and watching you move. You are so *strong*, my girl. One day we got a shipment of meat from Wild Pastures, and you wanted to move the box from the front porch to the kitchen counter all by yourself. The box was pretty heavy — 15 or 20 pounds — but more than that, it was bulky, which was significant for your little arms and body, but you did it! You maneuvered your arms around that box, picked it up, and lifted it higher than your waist to put it up on the counter. I was proud and impressed by your determination.

After CrossFit class, you were dirty — your knees especially, probably from the burpees you did during the workout. Both you and Michael resist showering for some reason at this age, so I suggested you and I shower together. Some people may see this as strange, and it might be, but I did it anyway, because I also needed a shower and I knew you'd say yes.

Once we were undressed, I caught you looking at yourself in the mirror, grinning as you rubbed your round belly. You saw me watching, and you turned around and started shaking your booty, delighting in watching it jiggle. You nicely pointed out how my boobs hang low, and invited me, "Mom! Jiggle your boobs!"

So I did! We laughed and laughed. I loved seeing how you love your body — and mine. You loving your own body helps me love my body, did you know that?  It's true. When we love ourselves, we love other people more easily, and that lets them see themselves as lovable.

Once we were in the shower and lathering up, I sounded a warning: "Athena, as you get older, some people are going to try and say that your body is shameful, and that it needs to be hidden, or covered."

Curiously, you asked, "Why?"

"Some people have different cultural or religious views that think the body is something shameful. But it isn't, Athena. Your body is absolutely amazing. That's not to say you go around walking naked wherever you want, obviously. Your body is *private*, not secret. That means *you* get to decide when to show it, how to show it, and to whom you show it.

"The important thing about anyone's body is *not* what it looks like. Do you know what it is, sweet girl?"

While rinsing off some soapy skin, you said, "That it's *strong!*"

"Pretty close, my love! What matters about someone's body is that it is *healthy,* so that they can do what they want to do!"

You love dogs, right? Dogs come in all shapes, sizes and temperaments. There are tiny Chihuahas, massive Mastiffs, lumbering Labs, medium mutts — and those variations serve them well. Some dogs love hunting, racing, or swimming. Some thrive in cold climates, others in warm.

Have you ever thought that all dogs should be the same? I'm guessing not. After all, if all dogs were like Pomeranians, our K-9 police forces wouldn't be very intimidating. If all dogs were like beagles, the world would be a very noisy place. If all dogs were the size of Wolfhounds, we'd need much bigger couches.

Doesn't it seem silly to think that all dogs should be the same size?

For instance, should we limit a Great Dane's food so that it can get down to the size of a Golden Retriever? Should a Dachshund try to reach the height of a Doberman?

The idea seems foolish, doesn't it? Almost laughable. Even if we tried, it wouldn't happen. It would actually harm the dog.

One last question to consider, sweet girl. Do dogs shame themselves because their body is not like other dogs' bodies? Of course not.

Yes, we want our dogs to be healthy so they can be our active and carefree companions for as long as possible. We feed them well so that they can run, jump, bark, and play happily, without letting weight or illness get in the way. But health does not equate to *one* body type or size. This goes for dogs, horses, cats, birds, reptiles, amphibians, fish, and just about any living creature you can imagine — including us.

Humans *also* come in various shapes, sizes and temperaments — and, guess what? Those variations also serve us well.  Just look at a marathon runner's body versus an Olympic weight lifter's body, or a gymnast contrasted to a linebacker in the National Football League. They are all healthy, despite being different sizes and shapes. Would any of them become *unhealthy* if they stopped exercising, stopped eating foods that helped them perform, stopped sleeping, and didn't manage their stress? The answer is yes, again regardless of size and shape.

It IS possible to be healthy and NOT be the same size or shape as other men and women around you. The messages of the media and the industries that profit from your insecurities would have you think otherwise, but we know better.

You love your pups no matter their shape and size. Can you say the same about yourself?

A person needs their body and brain to be able to perform to the best of its unique ability, because that is how each person can live a rich, full life of purpose — however they choose to spend it.

This doesn't mean that we all need to be runners, weightlifters, or elite athletes. This doesn't mean that people like Papa in a wheelchair, or those battling cancer, or anyone with a brain irregularity or body deformity are any less important or valuable. No, it means, they, too, need to provide their brains and bodies with the best nutrition and lifestyle they can, to maximize their experience. They often know better than anyone that how they treat and feed their bodies matters.

All of us have to start with our bodies and brains the way they are, and work with what we've got. I've got scoliosis, and my particular case means my spine not only curves in an "S" shape in two different spots, it also rotates forward on one side. Consequently, I experience a decent amount of chronic pain, and it limits some of my movements, but I do what I can to keep my body as strong and healthy as possible. I've been told multiple times that if I didn't have as much muscle mass as I do that my spine would be more bent than it already is.

A nice quote to live by is the one attributed to Helen Keller: "Be happy with what you've got while working for what you want." That's what I want for you, my sweet girl: a life lived on *your* terms, not limited by your body, but *enhanced* by your body's health, and what it can do for you. Your body is your one vehicle to enjoy this wonderful and priceless adventure we call life, Athena. Respect and honor it. You *are* body beautiful.

# Afterword: Words of Love

D ear Athena,

When I was turning 30, I was in love with a guy, and I thought he was the one. I wanted him to be the one, but he wasn't.

He was at my 30th birthday party, which was 18 years ago at the time of this writing, and so were my parents. There's a picture of my dad hugging me that night that I treasure: I'm leaning in, my arms around him; one of his arms is around my back, and the other hand is palming the back of my head. You can see his face, but not mine. His eyes are closed, he has his beard, and his mouth is open in a big, wide grin, making his dead front tooth very prominent (when I was a girl, I called it his gold tooth, and he told me he always knew I had drawn a picture of him because I always colored one of his teeth gold).

Around that time, I was introduced to the work of Gary Chapman, a well-known marriage counselor and psychologist who has discovered that people express love in five main ways, which he deems our love languages.[47]

I've shared them with you before, do you remember? They are:

1. Physical Touch

2. Giving and Receiving Gifts

3. Words of Affirmation

4. Spending Quality Time

5. Acts of Service

It's worth repeating that I find these types of insights helpful, because it's only when we become aware of our own behaviors and tendencies that we can do anything about them, whether that be cultivate them, change them, or channel them. If we remain unaware, they become blind spots, unknowingly running our lives, limiting our power, vision, and possibilities.

We've discussed these Love Languages before, mostly when trying to explain why you and Michael sometimes butt heads, or say the other one doesn't love you. It's not that they don't love you, it's that they speak a different love *language* than you. They show love, and receive love, in different ways than you do.

What's interesting is that most of us end up with partners and family members who speak different Love Languages than we do, and therein begins the conflict.

If we don't think the other person loves us — well, we don't feel loved, do we? But, if we learn that other people are simply expressing their love for us in ways that *they* understand, then we can see them for what they are: demonstrations of love for us. We can communicate our love language, as we learn to speak theirs.

I had just finished reading Dr. Chapman's book when my parents came to visit me in Beaverton for that 30th birthday party my friend Stef was hosting. I was contemplating what my love language was when my parents arrived.

As if they were acting out a planned performance, my mom walked in the door and announced, "Darlin'! Let's go shopping. We need to get you some new clothes."

Gifts! Your MeeMa is a great gift giver, and always has been. She loves giving gifts. She loves giving gifts so much that once, many years ago, she gave my dad a gift that she wanted for herself, but couldn't trust anyone to get it for her — so she bought it, and gave it to my dad for Christmas. What was it? A beautiful dolphin statue that my dad had absolutely no interest in, whatsoever. It's a family joke now, and we wonder who might get a "dolphin gift" this year. Dolphin gifts aside, MeeMa truly does love giving gifts. Have you noticed how every time she comes to visit, she comes bearing an entire suitcase full of them? That's her, showing us love in her language.

Well, that day, my mom and I returned from our shopping spree, loaded with bags from Ross and TJ Maxx (because my mom loves sales and discount stores; who doesn't?), and my dad proudly greeted us with *his* announcement: "Okay! I replaced your light bulb in the bathroom that was out, I mowed the lawn in the back, and took Amos out to play fetch for a while." Acts of service — that was my dad showing love in ways that he understood.

Once I knew this about him, I remembered all the other times he had shown me love: building spice racks for my mom and brothers (which I still use and treasure), making my college roommate Debbi and I our desk/loft beds (way before they were trendy), making me a picnic table, building Amos's dog house, and spending an entire weekend of physical labor redoing my front and backyard with me.

Their love languages were very clear. I had a hard time figuring out mine, though. Was I acts of service, too? I loved baking and giving goodies to people. Was I quality time? Physical touch? I didn't know. I certainly wasn't gifts or words of affirmation.

I finally learned the answer 12 years later, when I was teaching my AVID students about the five love languages. I was also able to identify your love language, and Michael's, too.

The questionnaire my students were completing gave examples of how children asked for love, and through that, I saw how Michael makes requests like, "Mom, come look at this." "Athena! Play this with me." "Dad, come here for a second." He's always asking one of us, or all of us, to play with him, to look at what he's done so he can explain it to us — that's quality time. Your brother understands he is loved when we spend time with him, when we do the things he wants us to do, and when we do those things *with* him. This love language may be why when he is angry, he withdraws and isolates himself in hopes of punishing *us* with *his* absence.

You, on the other hand, are quite content to be alone. You play alone very well, entertaining yourself with crafts, toys, and music. What you ask for is cuddle time, hugs, and kisses. That's physical touch. When you were four, your neighbor friend Lydia was going home, and you went in for a hug, like usual. However, she didn't want to hug you back. You cried and cried, saying she didn't like you, but really, it was that your love language was physical touch, and hers wasn't. This could be why now, when you're angry, you run away — not to be alone, but to deprive me of the chance to hug you, because you think that will hurt me.

You both have secondary love languages. Michael's is physical touch, and yours is words of affirmation. You constantly give compliments, encourage others in their pursuits, and tell them how great they are doing with it. Even teachers (and they're not always your direct teachers!) have told me how good you make them feel, by explaining what wonderful people they are. This could also explain why when you are angry, you spew words of hate to the people closest to you, explaining that they are terrible people, that they are "the worst!"

Isn't that interesting? We withhold love in the way that we understand it, but if it's not in the same language as the person who offended you, it doesn't hurt them — it only hurts us.

Back to my classroom. Indirectly, my students helped me figure out my love language. Each time I would speak to a student individually, telling him or her how incredible I thought they were as people, pointing out all the qualities I saw in them — I would inevitably start crying. It was embarrassing! I eventually put the pieces together and realized that my love language is words of affirmation — which is exactly the one I always thought I *wasn't*. If I'm honest, I suppose I didn't deem it as substantial a love language as the other four; it just seemed so *fluffy*.

However, words have great power (as I also explained in Chapter 20). If you believe in the Bible, there are multitudes of verses that speak of the power words hold, and caution us to use our words wisely, reminding us of their influence:

- "In the beginning was the Word, and the Word was with God, and the Word was God."[48]

- "And God said, 'let there be light, and there was light."[49]

- "From the fruit of his mouth a man's stomach is filled; with the harvest from his lips he is satisfied. The tongue has the power of life and death, and those who live it will eat its fruit."[50]

- "What goes into a man's mouth does not make him 'unclean', but what does out of his mouth, that is what makes him 'unclean'."[51]

My understanding is that most world religions also believe our words are full of energy, and therefore, highly powerful.

Yet we are also taught the opposite, that actions speak louder than words, and the childhood saying, "Sticks and stones may break my bones, but words will never hurt me." I'm guessing that those phrases were coined by people whose love language was acts of service or gifts, because it turns out, words *do* matter, at least to me.

Whenever I speak words from the heart (or read words from the heart others have written), tears well in my eyes. That's probably why I struggle so much when you and Michael get angry and tell me, "You're the worst, mom!"

It's hard to separate my emotions from my personal love bank.

If my love language is words of affirmation, it might also explain why I love books and languages so much. I love how changing only one word, or a single punctuation mark, or the verb tense, can change the entire meaning of a sentence, or the tone of an entire passage. It could also be why I wanted to write this book. Words help me process, but they are also a way for me to express my love to you, to all people; to communicate how I feel.

I appreciated this passage that I read in Jodi Picoult's book *Change of Heart*, in which a character, Father Michael, is explaining how there are many life experiences we cannot name, like birthing a child, or losing a loved one, or falling in love. He says,

"Words are like nets — we hope they'll cover what we mean, but we know they can't possibly hold that much joy, or grief, or wonder... If it's happened to you, you know what it feels like. But try to describe it to someone else, and language only takes you so far."[52]

Sweet girl, I never knew how little I loved myself until I had you. When I learned I was having a girl, I was afraid history would repeat itself. I didn't want a self-loveless life for you. I wanted you to live a vibrant life, believing in and trusting yourself. I didn't want a distant relationship with you. I wanted us to *be* close, and to *stay* close, for the duration of our lives. I didn't have a model for any of that, and I agonized that I would fail.

*Your* birth was the beginning of *my* redemption. Seeing how you loved yourself innately allowed me to begin to love myself. *You* were the catalyst for my healing. You are the reason I began reclaiming my power and worth from all the spaces and places I had left it behind, throughout my past. Now, I get to create a loving and caring relationship with my own mom, with my daughter, *and* with myself. Now, I get to live powerfully.

When the idea for this book was still in its infancy, I was visited by an ancestor. A woman, who I believe to be my great-great grandmother. She was silent and still, yet strong. She was beckoning me, and this project, forward while staying grounded where she was. I felt a sizzle of connection, and an awareness that I come from a long lineage of women, all powerful, yet perhaps not all realized it. I understood that the women who came before us are part of our heritage, yes, but also part of our destiny. It's up to us to not only step into our power and strength, but to carry it forward.

I share these words with you because the love you have for yourself now — I wish for you to cultivate it, and keep it with you forever. It's so easy to internalize the negative experiences we have in our lives and give ourselves away to them, little by little, piece by piece, each time diminishing our self-worth and power, forgetting who we are, or where we originated. I don't want that future for you. I want you to grow in your power, to flourish in your capacity, to blossom in your strength — not only in love, but also in impact.

Will my words help? It's hard to say; they're merely words, not actions — you must do that part yourself. Being a parent (and a teacher) sometimes feels like watching a redwood tree grow. Regardless, I must try. I hope these words of love reach you, my sweet, tenacious, precious girl — and every other person who reads them. They truly are written *for* you, from me, but also *for and from* you. We are from, and for, one another. One day you might have a daughter, and she would be both from and for you, just as she would be for and from me. So would your son. Mysteriously and inexplicably, we are all connected.

Loving yourself will amplify your love for the people around you, and your love for life, Athena, just as it has for me. Loving *you* has finally allowed *me* to love myself again — *and* my mom. *Thank you* for such an indescribably priceless gift.

With love, even more than words can possibly say,
Mommy

"And all the colors I am inside
Have not been invented yet."[53]
-Shel Silverstein


"Look at the sky: that is for you. Look at each person's face
as you pass on the street: those faces are for you. And the
street itself, and the ground under the street, and the ball of
fire underneath the ground: all these things are for you."[54]
-Miranda July

# Acknowledgments

I have wanted to write a book for many years, but never knew what that book might be. Thanks to Bo Eason and his pre-conference coursework, I figured that out. While preparing for his Personal Story Power Event, these memories came tumbling out, along with an urgent desire to compile them purposefully as lessons learned along the way to share with my daughter. Without his prompting, these memories would still be waiting to burst forth. I'm grateful to his team members Jeffrey, Colleen, Mary, and Dawn for their unique contributions to my stories and their confidence in the impact those stories will make.

I must acknowledge the divine inspiration that accompanied that pre-coursework, and thank the heavens/ angels/ spirits that presented me with the idea. Millions of women could have written a book like this, and their stories would be just as compelling as mine, if not more so. But, like Elizabeth Gilbert explained in her enchanting book *Big Magic*, for some reason, the idea landed on me, vividly and clearly, and in me found a willing recipient. I feel deeply humbled to be a vessel of this message, and hope to fulfill on that duty.

A heartfelt and special thank you to Kim Harris, Stefanie Kingston, and Emily Gleason for reading through the original manuscript for this book. Your keen eyes, astute observations, syntactical suggestions and recommendations were absolutely needed. Each of you gave specific insights that, after implementing, made the book much more cohesive and impactful. Even more than your insights on the book, my friendships with you are true blessings in my life and I'm grateful for you. To Jen Grumbling, your willingness to read my draft gave me assurance that someone I didn't know very well might be interested in the book.

To Sarita Laroche, an enormous thank you for your willingness to share your knowledge and experience in book publishing with me. Your energy, generosity, and time was a tremendous boost — not only to my learning curve speed, but also my psyche. You are much appreciated.

To my advance readers, you are an incredible group of powerful women. DeeDee Fitch, the honest emotion and wisdom infused into your comments and review of the book hit me in the heart. Courtney Florez, I'm grateful for your honest input on possibly the most debated chapter (and definitely the most often revised), as well as the authentic example you set for your daughters and all women. Brooke Mattern, you tell it like it is, a trait I respect. I appreciate you offering your view amidst the many plates you juggle so well. Laura Magdalen, your enthusiasm and passionate support for not only reading my book, but promoting it, was critical to my belief. Sidra Jeffries, I value your perspective as an avid reader and insights as fellow mom. Holly Starr, your heartfelt words prompt people's best efforts and lift their eyes towards greater heights. Liudmila Wilson, the poignant, articulate prose you used to respond to my questions describes the very heart of this book, and journey of every woman. Ashleigh Anderlik, I love how you keep it real, fun, and show up for both yourself and your daughters. Plus, you look great in shorts. Vanessa Pinkham, mystical mermaid of the land, I admire all you do to strengthen women and men of this world and keep us well-rounded. Lisa Sprague, the love and joy you infuse into life is evident, even when you're down under. Thank you all for your support of this book, and who you are to me.

To Stephanie Warren, mama of two boys and two girls, and the first to believe in my ability to cultivate a close relationship with my own daughter, I needed that infusion you gave. It offered hope I carry with me still.

To my cherished readers, it is *your* lives that inspire the words on these pages. Your own struggles and support fuel my passion, and I'm deeply grateful for your presence on this journey. I truly believe we are in this together, and my hope is that we are for one another in life. If you feel this book would help another woman on her voyage, please, recommend it or pass it along. I hope this book serves as a reminder of the profound love we owe to ourselves *and* the future generation, igniting a pursuit of self-discovery and empowerment in each of us. May your lives become masterpieces you embrace with joy each day.

To my dad, Mike, for showing me your version of a really great dad. How you would have *delighted* in your five grandchildren. Although I wish I could've had you for longer, I was fortunate, lucky, and blessed to have you for 34 years. It's my honor to carry on the pancake breakfast tradition every weekend. The memories I have with you are more priceless than the world's greatest treasure. I love you and miss you always.

To my mom, Carolyn, whose strength and resilience have inspired me greatly. You are resolute in your love for your children, and your generosity knows no bounds. Despite our distant past, I've come to deeply respect and admire the woman you are. Welcoming you into our home in your later years is an honor I cherish. Your presence enriches our lives, and I'm grateful for the opportunity to care for you with the love and respect you deserve.

To my brothers, Chris and Todd, who have always been sources of support in my life. Despite the inevitable ups and downs, your presence and guidance have shaped me in countless ways. Our memories together are treasures to me. I cherish our relationships, and always look forward to seeing you both.

To Michael, my incredible son. Your youthful spirit embodies wisdom beyond your years. Your curiosity and determination inspire me daily, reminding me of the joy in lifelong learning and growth. Your compassionate heart and colorful soul illuminate our lives, teaching me invaluable lessons in love and empathy. I am endlessly proud of the remarkable person you are becoming. I absolutely love being your mom.

To Athena, my fierce daughter. You are a force of nature. Your tenacity and intelligence shine brightly, illuminating paths others may overlook. Embrace your unique brilliance and trust your inner strength, for you are not defined by anyone else's expectations. Your independent spirit and boundless creativity remind me daily of the potential we all hold within. I love being your mom, too.

To my favorite person and husband, Ben, my unwavering ally and greatest champion. You're the best. Your steadfast support and unfailing belief in me have ignited a fire within my soul. From the moment we met, you saw the real me inside. It's your vision that has inspired me to believe in myself and my ability to affect change. I'm proud of you as a father, and grateful our children have your belief as a foundational pillar for their own.

No matter what they choose to do, who they become, or where they go, you're on their team. I cherish every moment by your side. I couldn't imagine this journey without you. I love you to the moon and back, and I don't ever want to leave you there.

# About The Author

Elisa Pool is an ex-teacher turned wellness enthusiast. After 19 years of public school teaching, Elisa left her career, her gym, and her house in Oregon so that she could travel the world with her husband, Ben, and their two children. After two years of nomadic life, they settled down for "normal" life in Florida. Elisa's favorite activities are reading and learning, being a mom to Michael and Athena, cooking nutritious meals for her family, and working out at her local CrossFit gym. She is host of the podcast, *Everyday Health, Simplified*, and her mission in life is to help other mamas love their brains and bodies so that their kids learn to do the same.

For free book club resources or a personal reflection workbook, please visit: www.elisapoolwellness.com/letterstomydaughter

To contact the author, please email: elisapoolwellness@gmail.com

Instagram: @elisapool_wellness

# Endnotes

1. Waheed, N. (2014). *Nejma*. CreateSpace Independent Publishing.

2. Waheed, N. (2014). *Nejma*. CreateSpace Independent Publishing.

3. Waheed, N. (2013). *Salt*. Self-published.

4. Oliver, M. (1992). *The summer day*. In New and Selected Poems, Volume One. Beacon Press.

5. Katie, B. (2003). *Loving What Is*. Three Rivers Press.

6. Rosenberg, J. (2019). *90 Seconds to a Life You Love*. Yellow Kite.

7. Taylor, S. R. (2018). *The Body is Not an Apology*. Berrett-Koehler Publishers, Inc.

8. Brown, B. (2021). *Atlas of the Heart*. Random House.

9. Rubin, G. (2017). *The Four Tendencies*. Harmony.

10. Riso, D. R., & Hudson, R. (1999). *The Wisdom of the Enneagram*. Bantam.

11. Urban, M. (2022). *The Book of Boundaries.* Random House.

12. Schucman, H. (1976). "Your task is not to seek for love, but merely to seek and find all the barriers within yourself that you have built against it." *A Course in Miracles, Workbook Lesson 155.*

13. Atwood, M. (2000). *The Blind Assassin.* McClelland & Stewart.

14. Ratey, J., & Manning, R. (2014). *Go Wild.* Little, Brown and Company.

15. Stevenson, S. (Host). (2024, February 27). *The Surprising Truth About Menopause & Lifestyle Changes for Menopause Symptoms — with Dr. Lisa Mosconi* [Audio podcast episode 769]. In *The Model Health Show.* Apple Podcasts. https://podcasts.apple.com/us/podcast/the-model-health-show/id640246578?i=1000647333747

16. Stevenson, S. (2020). *Eat Smarter.* Little, Brown Spark.

17. Gladwell, M. (2019). *Talking to Strangers.* Little, Brown & Company.

18. Rhimes, S. (2015). *The Year of Yes.* Simon & Schuster.

19. Kwik, J. (2020). *Limitless.* Hay House Inc.

20. Clear, J. (2018). *Atomic Habits.* Avery.

21. Hardy, B. (2018). *Willpower Doesn't Work.* Hachette Books.

22. Landmark Worldwide. (n.d.). *The Landmark Forum and/or the Advanced Course.* Retrieved from www. landmarkworldwide.com

23. Stevenson, S. (Host). (2022, October 4). *Why Mismanagement of the Human Mind Is Creating a New Mental Health Epidemic — with Dr. Caroline Leaf* [Audio podcast episode 623]. In *The Model Health Show.* Apple Podcasts. https://podcasts.apple.com/us/podcast/the-model -health-show/id640246578?i=1000581620920

24. Stevenson, S. (Host). (2022, October 4). *Why Mismanagement of the Human Mind Is Creating a New Mental Health Epidemic — with Dr. Caroline Leaf* [Audio podcast episode 623]. In *The Model Health Show.* Apple Podcasts. https://podcasts.apple.com/us/podcast/the-model -health-show/id640246578?i=1000581620920

25. Pressfield, S. (2011). *The Warrior Ethos.* Black Irish Entertainment.

26. Amen, D. (2022). *You, Happier.* Tyndale.

27. Eason, B. (2019). *There's No Plan B for Your A Game.* St. Martin's Press.

28. Brown, B. (2010). *The Gifts of Imperfection.* Hazelden.

29. Waheed, N. (2013). *Salt.* Self-published.

30. Ratey, J., & Manning, R. (2014). *Go Wild.* Little, Brown and Company.

31. Shenk, D. (2010). *The Genius in All of Us.* Anchor Books.

32. Ellenhorn, R. (2020). *How We Change.* Harper Collins.

33. Kwik, J. (2020). *Limitless.* Hay House Inc.

34. Lipton, B. (2015). *The Biology of Belief.* Hay House Inc.

35. Shenk, D. (2010). *The Genius in All of Us.* Anchor Books.

36. Stevenson, S. (Host). (2022, June 7). *How Your Beliefs Control Your Biology – with Dr. Bruce Lipton* [Audio podcast episode 590]. In *The Model Health Show.* Apple Podcasts. https://podcasts.apple.com/us/podcast/the-model-health-show/id640246578?i=1000566178886

37. Shenk, D. (2010). *The Genius in All of Us.* Anchor Books.

38. Mosconi, L. (2018). *Brain Food.* Avery.

39. Amen, D. (2022). *You, Happier.* Tyndale.

40. Amen, D. (2022). *You, Happier.* Tyndale.

41. Brown, B. (2021). *Atlas of the Heart.* Random House.

42. Robbins, M. (2021). *The High Five Habit.* Hay House Inc.

43. Rosenberg, J. (2019). *90 Seconds to a Life You Love.* Yellow Kite.

44. Leaf, C. (2021). *Cleaning Up Your Mental Mess.* Baker Books.

45. Shenk, D. (2010). *The Genius in All of Us.* Anchor Books.

46. Kennedy, B. (2022). *Good Inside.* Harper Collins.

47. Chapman, G. (1995). *The Five Love Languages.* Moody Publishers.

48. Biblical Citation: John 1:1, New International Version

49. Biblical Citation: Genesis 1:2, New International Version

50. Biblical Citation: Proverbs 18: 20-21, New International Version

51. Biblical Citation: Matthew 15:11, New International Version

52. Picoult, J. (2008). *Change of Heart*. Atria Books.

53. Silverstein, S. (1976). *Where the Sidewalk Ends*. Harper & Row.

54. July, M. (2007). *Majesty*. In M. July, *No One Belongs Here More Than You*. Scribner.

Made in the USA
Las Vegas, NV
09 May 2024

89731635R00154